The Wonderful Thing about Pets

The Wonderful Thing about Pets

*Remarkable stories about the animals
who share our lives*

FROM

GARY BURGHOFF

and the editors of

Pets
part of the family™

Edited by Christian Millman

RODALE

Pets: Part of the Family public television series is generously underwritten by PETsMART, PETsMART.com, and Fresh Step cat litter.

Pets: Part of the Family is a trademark of Rodale Inc.

Printed in the United States of America on acid-free ∞, recycled paper ♻

Library of Congress Cataloging-in-Publication Data

Burghoff, Gary.
    The wonderful thing about pets : remarkable stories about the animals who share our lives / from Gary Burghoff and the editors of Pets, part of the family ; edited by Christian Millman.
       p.   cm.
    ISBN 1–57954–187–9 hardcover
    1. Pets—Anecdotes. 2. Pet owners—Anecdotes. 3. Human–animal relationships—Anecdotes. I. Millman, Christian. II. Pets, part of the family (Firm) III. Title.
    SF416 .B87   2000
    636.088'7—dc21   99–089629

Distributed to the book trade by St. Martin's Press

2   4   6   8   10 9 7 5 3 1   hardcover

Visit us on the Web at www.petspartofthefamily.com, or call us toll-free at (800) 848-4735.

---OUR PURPOSE---

To explore, celebrate, and stand in awe
before the special relationship between us
and the animals who share our lives.

Pets
part of the family™

The Wonderful Thing about Pets Staff

EDITOR: Christian Millman
PRINCIPAL WRITERS: Bill Holton, Cynthia Miller
CONTRIBUTING WRITERS: Sheree Crute; Linda Formichelli;
Joanne Howl, D.V.M.;
Nancy Lawson; Karin B. Miller;
Jana Murphy; Lee R. Schreiber;
Selene Yeager
ASSOCIATE ART DIRECTOR: Charles Beasley
COVER AND INTERIOR DESIGNER: Joanna Williams
COVER AND INTERIOR ILLUSTRATOR: Greg Dearth
COVER PHOTOGRAPHER: Shel Secunda
RESEARCH MANAGER: Leah Flickinger
EDITORIAL RESEARCHER: Holly Ann Swanson
SENIOR COPY EDITORS: Susannah Hogendorn,
Karen Neely
EDITORIAL PRODUCTION MANAGER: Marilyn Hauptly
LAYOUT DESIGNER: Donna G. Rossi
ASSOCIATE STUDIO MANAGER: Thomas P. Aczel
MANUFACTURING COORDINATORS: Brenda Miller, Jodi Schaffer,
Patrick T. Smith

Rodale Active Living Books

VICE PRESIDENT AND PUBLISHER: Neil Wertheimer
EXECUTIVE EDITOR: Susan Clarey
EDITORIAL DIRECTOR: Michael Ward
MARKETING DIRECTOR: Janine Slaughter
PRODUCT MARKETING MANAGER: Kris Siessmayer
BOOK MANUFACTURING DIRECTOR: Helen Clogston
MANUFACTURING MANAGERS: Eileen Bauder, Mark Krahforst
RESEARCH MANAGER: Ann Gossy Yermish
COPY MANAGER: Lisa D. Andruscavage
PRODUCTION MANAGER: Robert V. Anderson Jr.
OFFICE MANAGER: Jacqueline Dornblaser
OFFICE STAFF: Julie Kehs, Mary Lou Stephen,
Catherine E. Strouse

• • •

For Baxter, Ollie, Calvin, Ming, Hero, Penny, Bowser,
Annabelle, and Boop

For Beauty, Walker, Fang, Gertrude, Boy, Mousie, Princess,
Speck, and Chuckie

For Kayla, Polly, Red, Sammy, and Winken,
Blinken, and Nod

• • •

*"When all other friends desert, he remains.
When riches take wing and reputation falls to pieces,
he is as constant in his love
as the sun in its journey through the heavens."*

—Senator George Vest, 1870

• • •

Contents

Contents

Contents

Contents

Contents

Contents

Contents

Introduction

Early on in my life, I spent a lot of time in the woods. It was easy, since I grew up in a place called Forestville, Connecticut, near Waterbury. In those days, Forestville lived up to its name.

My constant companion on those sojourns into the deep timberland was my dog Patch. Patch was my best friend. With him, I learned of the incredible richness of life all around us. I watched the animals in the forest and looked in awe at the profound relationships they had with each other and the land.

From Patch, I learned the meaning of unconditional love. Oddly, it was years later that I fully realized this. I left home at the age of 19 to attend acting school in New York City. At one point, we were asked to do an advanced acting exercise called sense memory.

The aim of this particular exercise was to lead us into an emotional state designed to bring on tears. I had to imagine something intensely personal and allow myself to get swept up in the grief of it.

Well, I tried a couple of things. I imagined my father being paralyzed. I saw myself being diagnosed with cancer. Nothing seemed to work. Then, even though I could hardly bear to entertain the thought, I visualized Patch being hit by a car.

To say that I became extremely emotional is almost an understatement. Why do you think that is? Well, I'll tell you. Of all the relationships that I had growing up, as important and as loving as they may have been, none gave me the completely unconditional love that Patch gave me. And I him.

You see, therein lies the true magic of our relationships with animals. That's what animals can teach us if we let them. Whatever the philosophical or sociological reasons, we humans find it difficult to practice unconditional love with one another.

But to find some of the best instructors on the planet, we need look no further than to the animals in our own homes. For some reason, we rarely fear the pets in our lives. And we admire them for the vulnerability that they show and the trust that they put in us. That's the same vulnerability that we're often afraid to show to the world around us.

But, I believe, that's the key to enhancing our human relationships as well. To me, this most valuable of lessons that we can learn from our pets can have a dramatic impact on the rest of our lives.

● ● ●

My Own Amazing Pets

In this book, you'll find an utterly astounding collection of true pet stories. I am joined in spirit with the people you'll read about because I have many of my own incredible stories to tell.

Let me tell you about when I first came to California.

I was renting a small house in Los Angeles in the early 1970s. One day, in the bushes behind the house, I found a small dog. She was so quiet and timid that, for the longest time, all I saw were her deep brown eyes. I named her Shy.

I began to feed her and, slowly, I gained her trust. Eventually, she came to live with me.

Well, on a February morning in 1971, Shy woke me up at five o'clock. She actually jumped on the bed and tried to push me out. Keep in mind that this was a timid dog who had never done anything like this. I tried to ignore her and go back to sleep. Immediately, she started shoving and pushing again. Finally, she grabbed my arm in her mouth and began pulling me out from under the covers.

And then a 6.7-magnitude earthquake hit. She knew an hour before it struck. She knew it before the world knew it. And she was trying to warn me. If you want more examples on the importance of listening to a pet when he urgently awakens you, read "A Bratty Cat Saves a Life" or "Duane and Goliath."

Then there was Chipper the squirrel. When I was a teenager, Chipper was orphaned near my house. He was barely weaned and the tiniest thing you ever saw. He was terrified of me at first and screamed every time I reached to comfort him.

Finally, I got the idea of putting on a fur-lined glove inside out. As soon as he felt the warmth of that fur, he bonded to me immediately. All he needed was the knowledge that he was safe and that I would care for him.

He stayed with me for more than 2 years, sharing my bed at night and playing in the trees during the day. But eventually, he reached full maturity. And, one day, we were outside together in the early autumn. He was up in a tree. A band of squirrels ran over to him, and a young female came halfway down the tree to meet him. Their noses touched, and Chipper's tail began to flash. I knew what was happening.

He looked at me and came down toward me. Then he ran back to his new friend. Once more, he came back down toward me as if to say goodbye. That was the last I saw of him, as he leapt through the treetops with his new family.

I'm not alone in knowing the strong bond that can be had between people and squirrels. Read "Rocky Meets His Bullwinkle" for a story on how that same connection made all the difference in the world to one man.

There are many other stories from the animals in my life. There's my dog Becky, who came with me to Toronto shortly after I left M*A*S*H, as part of some work I was doing for a pet-food company. She blew people away with her mathematical abilities.

And Flippy, my cat, used to dive under water to catch fish. Flippy actually caused me a lot of grief because nobody believed that a cat would do that. Finally, someone else saw it, and I was vindicated.

But for now, I'd like to leave you with the rest of the stories in this book. Read them, be amazed by them, but, above all, learn from them. Learn that there is so much more to animals than we often realize. Learn that pets can teach us as well as we teach them. Learn that love, trust, and laughter are what makes it all worthwhile.

Enjoy.

Gary Burghoff
Host of *Pets: Part of the Family* television show

The Wonderful Thing about Pets

chapter one

The Overflowing of Juggy's Cup

*I*magine for a moment the life of a stray dog. Cold, hungry, abandoned on the streets, lonely.

Now imagine that you've taken her in, given her shelter, food, and love. It's no surprise that somehow the dog senses your kind heart and compassion. She understands that you probably saved her life, and she will often spend the rest of that life devotedly trying to repay your love and generosity in kind.

And then there are dogs like Juggy—dogs who accept your love and then find a very special and unique way to pass it on.

The first several times that Doris Bryant saw Juggy, she couldn't tell for sure whether the animal was a dog, a raccoon, or a coyote. Every time that Doris walked out the front door of her Fredonia, Kansas, home, she would glimpse just the tip of a furry tail disappearing around the side of the house.

But then, one day, cold and hunger finally overcame inhibitions. On a frosty November morning, when Doris stepped out onto her porch, the stray didn't run off. Instead, she stood huddled in a far corner of the yard, eyeing Doris with a mixture of fear and just a tiny bit of hope. The stray was a stumpy-legged beagle mix with no tags dangling from her dried-out leather collar.

"In my whole life, I've never seen such wide, sensitive eyes on either human being or beast," says Doris. "They were tragic yet kindly, apologetic yet sparkling."

There's a lakefront recreation area a short way up the road from the Bryants' home, and Doris figured that the pup had been abandoned by some vacationers. "Are you hungry?" she asked, taking a tentative step toward the stray.

When the beagle didn't run off, Doris moved closer. Their eyes locked. "When a dog meets your eyes like that, it usually means one of two things," says Doris. "Either she's going to love you, or she's about to attack you." Happily for Doris, the

answer quickly became evident. "As I got closer, she started wagging her tail," says Doris.

Doris went inside to fetch a plate of food. The stray gobbled it down as if it were her first decent meal in weeks, which it probably was. The next time that Doris came outside, the pup was back for more. Before long, she began waiting for Doris on the sheltered front porch.

● ● ●

Juggy Begins a New Life

When no one stepped forward to claim the stray, Doris and her husband, Robert, decided to adopt her. "We named her Juggy because she looked like one of those earthenware cider containers when she sat upright on her haunches to beg," Doris says.

Doris took Juggy to a veterinarian for shots and spaying. According to the doctor, Juggy was 6 or 7 years old and had been a mother many times.

Indeed, Juggy turned out to be an extremely motherly type of pet, always concerned with the safety and well-being of her new family. She was an excellent guard dog, barking firm warnings whenever a stranger approached but never biting anyone. She followed Doris everywhere, and whenever the Bryants took their boat out fishing on the nearby lake, sooner or later they'd spot Juggy, watching them from the shoreline, her big brown eyes all but pleading, "Can I come, too?"

Robert found an old wooden packing crate and tipped it sideways on the front porch. He filled it with blankets and installed a heat lamp over the crate, which they switched on when the temperature dipped near zero and the Kansas nights grew windy.

Almost immediately, Juggy began to forgo the blankets in favor of climbing atop the crate and stretching out beneath the warm bulb. But with her short legs, it was quite an endeavor for Juggy to climb up and down from the 3-foot crate. So Doris decided to save Juggy a few steps by placing her food dish atop the crate beside her. Every night, she fed Juggy a can of dog food.

Before too long, Doris and Robert began to notice a most peculiar behavior.

● ● ●

What Goes Around, Comes Around

Every night, when Doris fed Juggy, the formerly unwanted stray would gobble down all of her food except for a tiny, walnut-size morsel, which she would leave on the edge of the bowl. Then, instead of stretching out beneath the heat lamp, the beagle would clamber down off the crate and curl up amidst her blankets for a while.

But by morning, Juggy would always be back atop the crate, lying beneath the bulb. And, strangely, the tiny morsel of dog food would always be gone.

The crate and light were just outside a window, so Doris and Robert spent several evenings patiently watching and trying to solve the mystery. One night, they found their answer.

Juggy ate her food, leaving the usual morsel. Then, as had become her custom, she climbed down off the crate and curled up inside it on the blankets. But it wasn't very long before another animal took Juggy's place standing on top of the old wooden crate.

"Look! It's a field mouse!" Doris exclaimed, when she recognized the tiny creature. The mouse raised its nose, its whiskers twitching as it sniffed the frosty winter air. Then it headed straight for Juggy's food dish. Quickly, the mouse ate its fill, then slipped down behind the crate and scampered off into the blustery winter night the same way it had come. Later still, Juggy climbed back onto the crate and stretched out as usual beneath the heat lamp.

"If this had happened only once or twice, Robert and I might have thought it was just a coincidence," says Doris. "But it happened night after night throughout that winter. My elderly parents witnessed the amazing sight. So did several of our friends and neighbors."

• • •

Viewing the World through Juggy's Eyes

Juggy knew what it was like to be cold and hungry. She also knew what it was like to find someone who cared enough to reach out a helping hand.

"I think this world is like a 3-D movie, but only a few of us ever take the time to put on the special glasses and really look around," observes Marty Becker, D.V.M., coauthor of *Chicken Soup for the Pet Lover's Soul*. "Those who do take the time are often rewarded with a glimpse of the interplay between species that's going on all the time, all around us."

According to Dr. Becker, most of our interaction with our pets occurs at times when we're the focus of the animal's attention—when we come home from work, or when we're playing with them or feeding them their dinners. "Only rarely do we stop and take the time to watch our pets go about their daily lives," he explains. "When we do, we're often delighted and astonished by what we discover."

Dr. Becker's own black Labrador retriever, Sirloin, can frequently be spotted galloping across his ranch, giving rides to

5

birds that have landed on his back. His cats rub up against his horses' legs, and, in turn, the horses play-chase the cats around the pasture.

Juggy's relationship with the field mouse was unique, but to Dr. Becker it isn't inexplicable. "Most living things beyond a certain level of consciousness have the same requirements that we do to love and be loved, to need and be needed," he says.

Many of us fulfill this need through our spouses or our children. Others of us fulfill it through our pets. Juggy fulfilled hers through a lowly field mouse, a tiny creature she could nurture, passing along just a bit of the love that Doris and Robert Bryant had given her. ✪

chapter two

An Unexpected Stay
with Bears

*A*ll of western Maine lay swaddled beneath a thick blanket of snow on a frosty February afternoon. Butch McCormick loaded four of his dogs into his pickup for a trip to the woods, a few miles from his home in the small town of Wilton.

It was a perfect winter's day to teach the dogs to hunt rabbits. Three of the pups proved to be quick learners, but the fourth, a small beagle named Dodger, seemed more interested in chasing his own shadow than rabbits.

"Dodger!" Butch called when it was time to load the hounds back into the truck and head home. But Dodger was nowhere to be found. The playful pup had wandered off into the dense underbrush.

Fortunately, the 3-year-old beagle was wearing a radio collar. And so, after dropping the other dogs off at home, Butch returned with his eldest son, Kevin. The two men used a homing device to track the collar's signal deep into the old-growth forest.

Butch and his son searched for several hours, but Dodger's trail eluded them. As the winter sun dipped below the horizon, they were forced to abandon the search. But Butch and Kevin returned the next day and the day after that.

Strangely, with every search, the radio beacon led Butch and his son directly to the very same spot in the woods. "He has to be within 30 yards of right here," Butch told Kevin, but search as they might, the two could find no sign of the missing hound.

● ● ●

Success . . . of Sorts

Then, on the fourth day, Butch climbed to the top of a thick pile of dried bramble, hoping for a better view. "Look!" he said, spotting a few faint tracks in the snow. They marked an entrance to a burrow that an animal had dug beneath the very pile of bramble where Butch now stood. "Dodger?" he called, and almost immediately, Butch and Kevin heard a faint rustling deep inside the deadfall.

"Dad, look—it's Dodger!" Kevin shouted as the hound's floppy-eared face poked a few inches outside the burrow entrance.

"C'mere, boy," Butch coaxed. But as Dodger scrambled to climb free, a huge, furry paw reached out and snatched him back inside. Butch and Kevin jumped back, surprised and a bit shocked.

It was a large, black bear, hibernating in her den for the winter with her two baby cubs. The groggy mama bear had mistaken Dodger for a cub and had forcibly adopted the beagle as one of her own.

Butch and his son knew better than to mess with a black bear. The species can reach 6 feet in length and weigh 500 pounds or more. And while black bears have never been known as man-eaters, there was no telling what a mother bear might do if she suspected that her young were in danger.

● ● ●

An Impromptu Rescue

Butch and his son hurried home and contacted Franklin County game warden Tom Jacobs, who returned with them to the scene of the adoption-abduction.

"Go ahead, call your dog," Jacobs said, and when Butch called out Dodger's name, the three men could hear the beagle whimpering while the baby cubs mewed like a pair of hungry kittens.

Jacobs, too, was wary of disturbing the mama bear without expert guidance. So the game warden contacted biologists from the state wildlife department, who agreed to help rescue the captive canine.

Wildlife biologists Sandy Ritchie and Allen Starr trekked into the woods carrying a jab stick, a 5-foot pole tipped with a tranquilizer dart. The plan was to sedate the mama bear long enough to free the not-so-artful Dodger and tag the bears for research purposes. But as the old saying goes, the best laid plans of mice and wildlife biologists . . .

Cautiously, Ritchie approached the den's opening, crouched low, and peered inside. To sedate the bear, she needed to stick the animal's rump with the tranquilizer dart. But to accomplish the task, first she had to determine exactly how the bear was oriented inside her den. Ritchie tried to be as quiet as possible so as not to rouse the dozing bear.

Unfortunately, Dodger had other ideas. By now, the hapless hound had been confined in the bear's den for more than 5 days, and he was understandably eager to be on his way.

The instant that he spotted Ritchie, he scrambled out from be-tween the noisily nursing cubs and tried to make good his es-cape. But mama bear wouldn't hear of such a thing. Every time Dodger jumped up, she swatted him back down with her paw. Meanwhile, Ritchie watched on, hoping for a clear shot at the bear's hindquarters.

But suddenly, Dodger lived up to his name and dodged the bear's paw. This time, he scrambled far enough out of the den to enable Ritchie to grab him by the collar. "I got him!" she exclaimed. But just then, the bear grabbed Dodger's back leg and began pulling in the opposite direction.

What followed has to be one of the most unusual games of tug-of-war on record. Ritchie pulled one way, and the bear pulled the other. Ritchie yanked. The bear yanked back. Dodger yelped, wriggled, and writhed, until eventually he threw off the bear's powerful grip and all but leapt into Ritchie's arms.

Free at last, Dodger didn't know what to do first. But there wasn't much time to decide, because a few seconds later, the mama bear followed him out of the den. But after a single look at the assembled group, she grew frightened and dashed off into the woods.

She didn't stay gone long. The next day, when Ritchie and Starr looked in on the cubs, their mom was back, snoozing contentedly while they suckled and mewed.

• • •

A Proper Adoption Takes Place

After more than 5 days of interspecies day care, Butch Mc-Cormick's pooch was pooped. He was also slightly dehy-drated. But when Ritchie checked inside his mouth, she caught a definite whiff of sour milk. Says Ritchie, "It's unlikely that a 3-year-old dog would have nursed, but bear cubs tend to be sloppy eaters, so it's likely that there was at least a little bit of leftover milk, which Dodger lapped up."

Dodger survived his ordeal with only a few minor tooth marks on his floppy ears. But as things turned out, Dodger may have saved the life of another bear cub several hundred miles away from the tiny den where Dodger had learned what it was like to be raised by an overprotective mother.

On Maine's Atlantic coast, a woodsman had inadvertently damaged a bear's den and frightened the mother away from her lone cub. Unlike Dodger's adoptive mom, however, this particular bear had failed to return once the coast was clear. Having heard the amazing tale of the beagle and the determined mama bear, local wildlife biologists decided nothing ventured, nothing gained. They transported the orphan to Franklin County, and bright and early the following morning, Sandy Ritchie snuggled the tiny cub inside her coat and carried it to the bear den.

The mama bear and her cubs had abandoned the den, but Ritchie and the others soon located their new home, less than a hundred yards away. Carefully, Ritchie placed the cub near the entrance. She barely had time to step away before a familiar, furry paw reached out and scooped the infant into the cozy darkness.

The last time that state wildlife officials looked in on them, mama bear and all three of the cubs were doing great. So is Dodger, although Butch McCormick has changed his mind and decided not to give him any more rabbit-hunting lessons. ❂

chapter three

One Cool Cat

You can call him Stanley Cup. You can call him Stanley Man. You can even call him Fats, and he'll know who you're talking to.

You just can't call him Fido, though you might be tempted to once you've read his story. Stanley Cup does all the things any well-trained pooch can do—and then some. He comes when called. He sits on command. He rolls over. He gives kisses.

He shakes paws. Turns around. Lies down. And, of course, like any self-respecting canine, he's leash-trained.

The thing is, Stanley Cup is no dog. He would probably even be offended if you so much as suggested that he was. He is, you see, a pudgy gray-and-brown tabby cat whose life began in the wild. The son of a stray, Stanley was brought to a veterinary clinic, along with his littermates, when he was just 3 weeks old.

After about 3 more weeks, Stanley fell into the lap of

luxury. Or, more exactly, into the lap of Gaye Kelley. Searching for a new pet kitten, Gaye called an animal clinic near her home in Grosse Pointe Woods, Michigan, and inquired as to whether employees were caring for any kittens in need of homes. She was in luck, and so was Stanley.

"He had the cutest little face, but he had this sort of rat tail—long and skinny with hardly any hair," says Gaye. "I had looked at other kittens, but I never felt that any of them were right. When I saw Stanley, I knew that he was the one."

* * *

School's In for Stanley

Stanley Cup—adopted on the same day that the Detroit Red Wings won the National Hockey League finals—is unique among cats, says Gaye. And she knows her felines. A lifelong cat lover, she collects cat knickknacks and figurines, reads *Cat Fancy* magazine faithfully each month, and pampers Stanley with kitty condos and toys galore.

It was this passion for felines—and a desire to learn everything she could about them—that led Gaye to some library books on cat training. Originally intending to study up on basic care, medical issues, and cat body language, she discovered that cats can be much more responsive to training than most people believe.

To Gaye, it only made sense. She had always known that cats were intelligent. Why would Stanley be an exception? Even as a young girl, she had been irked by some people's claims that cats weren't as smart as other pets. One look at Stanley planning a strategic attack on a fly, she says, and you know that there's some type of mental calculation occurring.

So, at the age of 6 months, Stanley began to give tricks a

try. And it worked. Before he was even a year old, Stanley starred in his first "feature film," a videotape made for the judges of the Michigan Humane Society's 1998 Smartest Pet in Detroit contest.

A second-place award and subsequent media appearances could have gone to their heads, but Gaye and her cat remain humble. She insists that the methods are simple and that Stanley is a quick study. (Stanley, if you ask him, is inclined to agree.) All it takes is a few treats, a lot of love, and one special kitty, she says.

Starting with the "sit" command, Gaye trained Stanley in much the same way that a dog trainer would teach his canine charges. After breaking soft cat treats into nibble-size pieces (so as not to make "Fats" any fatter), she would say, "Sit," and gently push Stanley's bottom to the floor, then give him a piece of treat. The method worked over and over again with other commands, until Gaye and Stanley completely emptied their bag of tricks.

"He caught on so quickly," says Gaye. "I couldn't think of anything else to teach him. I tried to get him to jump from chair to chair, but he's not a jumper. He'd just sit there and look at me like, 'No. Absolutely not. I don't care how many treats you bribe me with. I am not going to jump around this house.'"

He may not jump, but Stanley will do just about anything else, even rolling over onto his back and exposing his belly. With his added girth, sometimes that trick requires a little extra help, so Stanley will extend his paw toward Gaye's pinky finger and get a little extra leverage for the ride over.

A polite kitty, Stanley likes to use his paws for gentlemanly handshakes as well, and he even knows his right from his left. "'Shake' is the left paw, and 'shake two' is the right paw," says Gaye. "If I put my hand down there and he gives me the wrong paw, I'll say, 'No,' and he'll give me the right one."

● ● ●

No Big Deal for Cool Cats

Gaye thinks for a moment when she tries to explain Stanley's accommodating behavior. Maybe he's just eager to please, she muses. Or maybe, she adds, laughing, he just loves his treats so much that he'll do anything to snag one.

Both of those explanations are probably true, says Scott Line, D.V.M., Ph.D., a veterinarian and animal behaviorist in Westfield, North Carolina, who operates a behavior referral practice for cat and dog owners. Because cats weren't bred the way dogs were—to be working animals with very specific behavioral characteristics—many people don't realize their training potential.

"A lot of people just haven't considered the possibility that their cat would respond that way, and so most people haven't tried it," says Dr. Line, who has also worked for the Animal Humane Society in Minneapolis and for the University of Minnesota. "But in working with different cats, I've found that there are some that will respond very quickly to these kinds of approaches and others that don't seem as interested or motivated. There's a lot of individual variability."

Tasty morsels can shape the behavior of a wide range of animals—even fish and birds, to a certain extent, says Dr. Line. But like their canine counterparts, cats are also susceptible to positive feedback from their humans—and they often crave it. "Cats and dogs like petting and praise and eye contact," Dr. Line says. "That social interaction can be very rewarding."

Social interaction is something that Stanley Cup understands very well indeed. Social butterfly that he is, he suffers no shortage of positive interactions with all sorts of species. He's even somewhat of a legend in his little corner of the world for his pleasing demeanor.

Although Gaye likes to keep him safely indoors, she sometimes lets him sit outside on a leash fastened to a clothesline, where he can get some fresh air and conduct meet-and-greet sessions with the neighbors. Keeping a watchful eye on him through the window, Gaye has often been stunned by the parade of visitors attracted to Stanley.

There are the little boys from the neighborhood who like to feed him one of his favorite treats: fish flies from a nearby lake. Then there's the roaming black cat who comes and touches noses with Stanley before settling peacefully down next to him.

Let's not forget the neighbor's kitten to whom Stanley likes to give baths. And, of course, there is Gaye's 86-year-old father, who sometimes jokes that he's going to fall and break a hip because Stanley likes to walk so closely in his shadow.

"Stanley is quite a character," Gaye says. "Everybody in the neighborhood knows him. Everybody likes him. People always say that he's special. He's very laid-back, very mellow. He's a people cat."

Stanley is so adaptable that he even loves car rides, an activity that sends most felines into fits of anxiety. Tagging along with Gaye when she shuttles her teenage sons around town, Stanley enjoys the trip to the pet supply store most of all. "I put him in the cart, and he sits there and looks around," she says. It's little surprise where his gaze most often falls: "He likes the fish a lot."

• • •

Stan the Man Kicks Back

It's certainly a rags-to-riches story for Stanley Man, who now finds himself lolling about in his collection of cat havens. From his hammock, a padded platform attached to a windowsill, Stanley can bird-watch in style. In his cat hut, a wicker dome with yet more padding inside on which to lounge, he can pretend that he's invisible. And from the top of his kitty condo, purchased with some of the money he won in the contest, Stanley can survey the grandness of his kitty kingdom.

Stanley has come a long way since the days when Gaye

first spotted his lonely face and hairless tail. But now, Stanley Cup's once-scraggly tail is full of fur, and he has grown into a pleasingly plump cat enjoying the good life.

And, perhaps most important, he has proved to the world that you don't have to be an animal of the pooch persuasion to know how to fool the humans into giving you some good chow.

"I wouldn't say that he's the most beautiful cat in the world," says Gaye, "but he's very special in other ways. And I wouldn't trade him for the most beautiful cat in the world. I wouldn't trade him for anything." ✪

chapter four

A Modern-Day Phoenix

*J*t was a frosty Sunday evening in February. Retired yacht captain Lynn Norley had just finished cleaning up after dinner. Well, why not watch a little television, she thought.

"Hi ya, Rupe!" squawked Lynn's 12-year-old African Grey parrot, Rupert, as she passed his cage in the dining room. She built a fire and cozied up on the living-room couch with her two dogs, a Doberman pinscher named Panther and a Jack Russell terrier named Alex.

It wasn't long before Lynn was snoozing in front of the television. At 10:30 P.M., she woke up, sleepily headed to the bedroom of her 250-year-old Pennsylvania farmhouse, and changed into a red flannel nightshirt. "Goodnight," she said to her animals.

Two short hours later, Lynn woke up again—this time to the sound of Rupert falling off his perch and clattering to the bottom of his cage. "This was not the first time Rupert had done this," says Lynn. "African Greys are not known for their coordination, and Rupert is no exception."

Normally, Lynn would hear Rupert climb back onto his perch and eventually settle down. But tonight was different. Tonight, Rupert's usual climbing sounds were replaced by noisy flutterings and a terrible squawking that grew louder and more frantic by the second.

Lynn came full awake. "Rupert must have hurt himself," she realized. Lynn climbed out of bed and threw on a robe. When she threw open the bedroom door, she gasped in astonishment and horror.

● ● ●

A Homeowner's Worst Nightmare

A sudden blast of heat scorched Lynn's eyes and nose. She couldn't see an inch: The entire house was filled with thick, acrid smoke. A faulty junction box in the kitchen had gone up in flames, and there were no smoke detectors in the pre–Civil War structure. Except, of course, for the fluttery, feathered kind.

"Birds are extremely sensitive to smoke and other airborne contaminants," says Michael Weiss, D.V.M., a veterinarian in Sewell, New Jersey. "When a bird inhales, the air not only fills the lungs, it also circulates throughout the body cavity, making the bird far more susceptible to respiratory distress and infections."

Pennsylvania coal miners, among others, used to carry canaries down into the mines for this very reason. Carbon monoxide and other poisonous gases would affect the birds long before they reached levels toxic to humans.

Meanwhile, Rupert's squawks were growing ever weaker. "I knew I had to get him out of that smoke right away," Lynn remembers. Bravely, she reopened the bedroom door and groped her way through the living room and into the dining room, where Rupert's large, wrought iron cage stood. Lynn found the cage, but the smoke was so thick that she couldn't find the door. And her lungs were burning; she was completely out of breath.

Fortunately, the heavy, oversize cage was on wheels. "I pulled Rupert's cage with one hand and followed the wall with the other until finally I found the dining-room door that led out onto the porch," she recalls. "I grasped the bolt, slid it back, pulled the door open, and gulped for air."

After filling her lungs with fresh air, Lynn located the cage door and pulled it open. She clutched Rupert to her chest and then ran back into her bedroom where the dogs were nervously pacing.

The very instant that Lynn slammed her bedroom door behind her, an explosion rocked the old stone house. "It sounded like a bomb had gone off," she says.

Despite the closed door, Lynn's bedroom quickly began filling with smoke. She grabbed her portable phone and made a quick dash for the safety of the bathroom. "Panther! Alex!" she called. The dogs quickly followed her in.

Lynn closed the bathroom door and jammed a towel in the threshold to try to ward off the toxic smoke. Then she tried switching on the portable phone to call 911. "It's not working!" she exclaimed.

Lynn still held Rupert cradled in her arms. But as she stood there, trying to decide what to do next, his wings began to flutter ever so weakly. The parrot gasped several times, and then his little body went limp, and his head drooped to one side. "My heart sank," says Lynn. "Rupert had warned me of the fire, and then he had died in my arms."

In rapid succession, several more explosions rocked the old stone house. "I have to get out of here!" Lynn thought. "There isn't any time."

• • •

A Friend Gets Left Behind

Lynn wrapped Rupert's body in her bathrobe and placed her old friend in the shower stall. Then she wet a shirt and pulled it over her head. "Come here, guys," she called to the dogs.

Carrying the Jack Russell under one arm and holding the Doberman by the collar, Lynn hurried across the smoky bedroom. The house had been constructed on a hillside; the main living area was on the second floor. But if Lynn and the dogs could make it to the long porch that ran the length of the house, they could climb down the steps to safety.

The instant that Lynn opened the bedroom door, however, she and the dogs were struck full force by a wave of flames and heat. Lynn cried out in alarm. The dogs howled. All three fled back across the bedroom toward the bathroom.

"There's no other way out," Lynn realized, studying the tiny bathroom window. She raised the sash and grabbed Alex. She held him out the window, lowering him as far as she could reach. She let go and hoped for the best.

Lynn followed the Jack Russell out the window and jumped. She struck the ground with a hard jolt. She checked herself and Alex over quickly; both were okay.

But Panther was still upstairs, trapped in the deadly inferno. As fast as she could, Lynn raced to the garage and fetched a ladder. Flames were licking at the roof as she propped the ladder against the bathroom window and climbed back inside.

"Panther doesn't like the bathroom because he associates it with baths, which he hates," says Lynn. "But that night, I didn't have to call Panther twice. I don't know how, but somehow I managed to pick him up—all 85 pounds of him. I hefted him over the sink and toilet and heaved him through the opening. Then I climbed back down. The dogs and I were both safe—thanks to Rupert."

● ● ●

A Savior Seems Lost

It was nearly 5:00 A.M. by the time firefighters had the fire fully under control. By then, there was little left of Lynn's historic home but scorched timbers and ashes. Arriving at her mother's house with the two dogs, Lynn told her mom, "We're okay, but Rupert is dead."

Later that same morning, Lynn and some friends returned to her house to see whether there was anything left to salvage. They also planned to bury Rupert—if they could find him. "I didn't care about anything that I had lost, except for Rupert," says Lynn.

Carefully, Lynn and her friends picked their way up what was left of the front stairs and made their way through the house and into the bedroom. Everything reeked of smoke, and the walls dripped with water from the fire hoses. Lynn fought back tears as she struggled through knee-deep debris to the bathroom where she'd last seen the parrot who had saved her life. The shower stall was filled with insulation, broken tiles, and scraps of charred wood. Rupert was entombed beneath the pile.

Lynn's friends offered to dig their way through to retrieve Rupert's body. Lynn waited in the bedroom while they slowly excavated the rubble.

Suddenly, one of the diggers cried out, "He's alive, and—ouch! He bit me!"

Lynn could hardly believe her ears. "I ran into the bathroom, and there he was," she says. "Pitch-black, soaking wet, and cold, but he was alive. I picked him up and stuck him under my shirt, and we raced to the vet's office. I kept saying over and over, 'I can't believe he's alive.'"

Like the mythical phoenix, Rupert had risen from the ashes. But just barely. Rupert was alive, but he was suffering from hypothermia, dehydration, smoke inhalation, and aspergillosis—a fungal infection that is often fatal to parrots and other birds.

But ironically, according to Dr. Weiss, who treated Lynn's parrot, "Being buried beneath that pile of rubble probably saved Rupert's life. The insulation and other debris protected him from the worst of the extreme heat, the icy fire-hose water, and then the subzero temperatures of that February morning."

Even so, for the next 3 weeks, Rupert's condition remained touch and go. On several nights, Dr. Weiss slept on the floor outside Rupert's cage to monitor his condition. Once, he had to give the parrot an avian version of a tracheotomy to keep him breathing.

But finally, one day, when Lynn arrived at the vet's office for a visit, Rupert greeted her with an enthusiastic "Hi ya, Rupe!" And a few afternoons later, Dr. Weiss discovered Rupert shouting, "Shaddup! Shaddup!" at a yapping dog. They began to sense that the parrot was going to be all right. Indeed, 3 weeks after Rupert saved Lynn's life, the parrot nonpareil was well enough to return with Lynn to her mother's house—but not before Dr. Weiss made a rather startling discovery.

Parrots have no external sex organs. During an exploratory endoscopic exam, however, the vet determined that Rupert wasn't a he; Rupert was a she.

A local newspaper sponsored a contest to give Rupert a new, more appropriate name. The winning entry was Sainte La Rupe, but Lynn still calls her feathered guardian angel Rupert. "Rupert still doesn't seem like a girl to me," she says.

Today, Lynn and Rupert visit schools as part of a fire safety lecture circuit. The kids love hearing Lynn tell the story of how Rupert saved her and her dogs from a fiery death, and how Rupert himself came back from the dead.

They also love listening to Rupert's newest trick—an ear-piercing imitation of a smoke-detector alarm. ✪

chapter five

A Funeral Home Goes to the Dogs

*I*n his 45 years as proprietor of Cooke's Funeral Home in Nitro, West Virginia, Fred Cooke has comforted thousands of grieving people. But in 1993, when his wife died of cancer, Fred was the one who needed comforting.

Fred's family and friends gathered round to offer their love and support. But there were so many lonely hours to fill.

"You should get a dog," Fred's daughter, Dorothea, suggested. "A dog might help you feel less alone."

Coincidentally, a friend's golden retriever had recently given birth. Fred fell in love with one of the rambunctious pups, took her home, and named her Abigail.

Abigail and Fred became constant companions. Fred was living in an apartment above the funeral home at the time, and every day he'd take his new best friend downstairs and let her play in his office while he worked. But then one day Abigail slipped out an open door and went looking for new friends to play with.

A Furry Shoulder to Cry On

Fred discovered Abigail in the chapel, curled at the feet of a woman seated in a chair near her husband's casket. Fred apologized profusely for the intrusion and reached over to lead Abigail away.

"Does she have to go?" the grieving widow asked him. "It's such a comfort having her here."

Soon, Abigail was sneaking out of Fred's office regularly and heading straight for one of the funeral home's visitation rooms. "She seems to sense who is most distraught, and those are the people she'll go to first," explains Fred. "She'll sit at their feet, perfectly still, and gaze up at them with those compassionate brown eyes of hers. And before you know it, they've stopped crying and started stroking Abigail's fur."

Consider it one of nature's kindest gifts to people. "Inside every dog there's a pointer who is able to point out that one person in a crowd who is in distress and who has an unmet or undermet need," says Marty Becker, D.V.M., coauthor of *Chicken Soup for the Pet Lover's Soul.* "Whether you're having a bad hair day or the doctor's just told you that you have only 6 months left to live, dogs have an uncanny ability to come to the problem and fill it with whatever it takes—never too much, always just the right amount."

"It's part of a dog's survival skills to be able to sense the emotional thoughts of others, especially those of more dominant animals, such as humans," explains Stephanie LaFarge, Ph.D., director of counseling services for the ASPCA. "Working alongside humans, dogs have been bred to sense and respond to nonverbal cues that we ourselves have been socialized to ignore or minimize."

An adult human encountering someone in tears may shy away, not wanting to invade that person's privacy. But a small child, unschooled in the ways of the world, might hurry over and offer up a much-needed hug . . . just like Abigail.

● ● ●

Part of the Family

In time, grieving families began to ask Fred if he could bring Abigail for a visit. "I remember one woman who was inconsolable," says Fred. "But then her children invited Abigail into the viewing room, and an hour later she'd slipped off her shoes and was nuzzling Abigail's tummy with her bare feet. Her children told me that it was the first time she'd calmed down since their dad died."

It's well-documented that stroking a pet has a number of positive physiological effects, Dr. LaFarge says, including lowering blood pressure, relieving anxiety, and even bolstering the immune system. "Somehow, we instinctively recognize that we will feel better if we pet that dog or cat," she says.

People crave touch, especially in times of strong emotional upheaval. "Usually, when another person touches you, there is the expectation that you will respond in a certain way," says Dr. LaFarge. "But there are times when we need that hug desperately, only we're not in a place where we can give back."

For Abigail, that's just fine. Like most dogs, she gives straight from the heart, expecting nothing in return but the opportunity to lend a much-needed hand.

Fred remembers one man who was having an extremely difficult time accepting his wife's death. "During the visitation, he couldn't sit still. He kept pacing and cursing like a sailor," says Fred. "But 15 minutes after Abigail came in, he was sitting on a couch scratching her behind the ears. When he got up to get a cup of water, he set another cup on the floor for Abigail, and when he returned to his seat, he made sure that there was enough room on the couch for Abigail to curl up beside him.

"The next day," says Fred, "Abigail stayed at that man's side throughout the funeral service. I don't think he could have gotten through it alone."

Abigail's one and only misstep occurred back when she was still a puppy, and even that turned out well. "She ate somebody's carnations," Fred explains with a smile.

Fred rushed out and bought fresh flowers, but the family wouldn't let him bring them in. "Aunt Mary was a real dog lover," they told him. "You can't imagine how it would have made her smile to see those chewed-up flowers."

Off duty, you won't find a more playful pup than Abigail. She loves to romp and chase sticks and mooch treats from

Fred's dinner plate. "But the moment she steps into that chapel, she turns into a completely different dog," says Fred. "She's quiet and respectful. I think she must have a sixth sense that tells her how to behave."

"Dogs feel most comfortable when they know their status—their place on the totem pole within the pack or the family," observes Dr. LaFarge. "One way that a dog learns his status is by having a job, a specific skill he can learn to master."

Some dogs are trained to be service dogs, police dogs, and the like. Others have to find their own career callings. Like most people, dogs enjoy performing tasks that they do well or that they have been praised and rewarded for doing.

Some dogs are good at spotting intruders and become self-appointed guard dogs for the home and property. Others flourish under the responsibility of watching the kids. Still others, like Abigail, work best in the language of the heart.

Today, Fred and Abigail are both semiretired, but Abigail still gets plenty of opportunities to do what she loves best. "I get frequent calls to help with the arrangements for family members I've known for decades," says Fred. "They tell me that I can come to the funeral, but only if I bring Abigail along." ✪

chapter six

The Whole World's a Stage

here are certain dogs in this world who just have more going on than the average pooch. They're a little smarter, a little cuter, a little better equipped to win over hearts. Some can cock their heads *just so* and melt butter. And some dogs are just so charming that you can't keep your hands off them.

Henri, an 11-pound, 11-year-old miniature dachshund residing in New York City, is one of those kinds of dogs. He's got spirit in spades and a devoted following to prove it. For the past 10 years, Henri, a canine model and actor, has charmed agents, trainers, producers, photographers, casting directors, and live audiences with his good looks and jaunty attitude.

But most important of all, Henri has charmed his owner, Martha Brdar, who says that having this dog has changed her life.

The Dream Dog

When Martha was a kid, she had two big dreams: to have a dog and to be a Broadway actress. It took the New York City native more than 30 years to realize her first dream. Oddly, the subject of her first dream helped her see that she no longer wanted the second.

"When I was a kid, I used to look at pictures of dachshunds, and I wanted one so badly," explains Martha. "But, honestly, everybody in my life, during my childhood and on into my adulthood, didn't want me to have dogs." When she was 34, Martha cast aside the opinions of "everybody" and made a deal with a breeder to buy a 9-month-old dachshund named Claude.

When Martha arrived to pick up her dog, she fell madly in love—with Claude's brother. "I was playing with Claude, and telling the owner, 'Oh, isn't he cute, what a nice dog,' and then I saw Henri," Martha recalls. "He was peeking around the corner, leaning like the Tower of Pisa, staring at me, and I thought, 'This is the dog, my dog. He's the dog I've been looking for my whole life.'"

Martha laughs now at the dramatic moment, but she knew then and there that she couldn't leave without taking the second dachshund, too. She coughed up the extra money for puppy number two and brought them both home.

Yes, they were brothers, but they had completely different personalities. Claude was sweet and reserved, with a shiny black coat and a fondness for naps in the sun. Henri had a disposition to match his red coloring—mischievous, fun-loving, and full of excitement.

Martha enrolled both dogs in an obedience class and was relieved that they quickly and easily absorbed the basic training. They could sit, stay, and come on command, and they were attentive to their owner's instructions.

It was Henri, though, who caught the eye of animal talent agent Linda Hanrahan of the Manhattan-based company, Animals for Advertising. Visiting the obedience school to scout for new talent, she was charmed by Henri's "star quality" and by his beauty. She was also impressed with his easy obedience.

She asked Martha if Henri might be interested in a little acting or modeling work on the side. Martha gave her their phone number. "I never expected to hear from her again," says Martha.

• • •

A Star Is Born

Henri and Martha heard from Hanrahan soon, and often. Within weeks, Henri was posing for photographers. His very first photo shoot resulted in a greeting card. From there, he moved on to shoots for the distinguished likes of the Saks Fifth Avenue catalog, *Mademoiselle*, *Allure*, and *GQ*.

But Henri's most unique and memorable role has been as a stage performer. He and Martha were having a ball with the modeling and acting gigs when Hanrahan called one day with the question that just about every actor would walk through fire to hear. "Would you like to do Broadway?" she asked.

"Oh yes, we would," Martha answered.

In August of 1996, Henri began rehearsals under Martha's guidance for Noel Coward's *Present Laughter* at the Walter Kerr Theatre in Manhattan. Henri's role was originally as little more than a prop. He would be carried onstage by a character and carried back off a moment later.

But the show's star, Frank Langella, was smitten with Henri and made a big fuss over the dog when he came onstage. Before long, the man and the dog were exchanging kisses. Langella began offering Henri a sip from his glass of Scotch (it was really tea), and Henri took to spicing up the show with an occasional bark or, better yet, a yawn while Frank was delivering his lines.

Backstage, Martha would prep Henri by wrapping him in his favorite blanket and running through his basic obedience commands. She would even brush Henri's teeth so he'd be sweet if Frank decided to kiss him.

It was during this time that Henri brought Martha to a crucial discovery. Over the course of 10 months spent accompanying Henri to the theatre and waiting backstage during his performances, Martha had the opportunity to get an up close and personal look at the life to which she'd always been drawn.

"It's funny," she says. "I've been acting for 20 years, and there have been all these things that I've wanted to do. Henri has done them. He took me to Broadway, and we had such a wonderful time, but I was able to see that it's not the life for me. Henri brought me there, then showed me that it's not what I want to do anymore."

When the show closed in June of 1997, Henri took the change in stride. "You know, on the last night of the show, they dragged me out onstage with him, and Frank introduced the cast," says Martha. "Henri barked like crazy as each cast member was introduced, and when they came to him, he just sat still and basked in the applause. I don't know how he could have known that they were clapping for him, but he did."

Success Hasn't Spoiled Him Yet

One thing that owners of animal actors rarely have to worry about is success going to their charges' heads. Animals just go along doing their jobs, happy to have a mission and pleased to find food in their bowls on schedule. Since fame hasn't turned Henri into a spoiled brat yet, Martha feels confident that it never will.

"The closest we came was after the Broadway show closed," she says. "He was used to getting a lot of attention and applause, and he was used to going to the theatre every day, too. For a few days, he kept going to the door, to the little dog bag that I carry him in, wanting to go. It didn't take him long, though, to figure it out. Then we both had some well-deserved rest."

• • •

A Consummate Professional

These days, the dachshund and his owner are pretty selective about their projects. "If he didn't love it, we wouldn't do it at all," says Martha, "but Henri still loves to work. His age hasn't slowed him down at all."

Like many an aging star, though, Henri does spend more time in the makeup chair than he used to. "We have to cover his gray for photo shoots," Martha notes. "But who cares?"

It is Henri's easygoing, cooperative manner, Hanrahan points out, that gets him the great jobs in the first place. "Henri has star quality," she says, "but it's more important how he takes it all in stride. If you take the average dog and set him in a basket and tell him to stay, like Henri had to when he had a role on *Saturday Night Live*, maybe he'll stay. But when you throw in a guy banging a drum beside him, two other dogs running around him, a band playing in the background, glaring stage lights, and a laughing live audience—that really separates the men from the boys, so to speak."

Hanrahan points out that owners who want their dogs to become performers usually make two false assumptions: one, that the pet will earn a living for both of them; and two, that being cute is enough.

"I have to tell them that there's more to it than that," says Hanrahan. "I can't use a dog who lies down when you tell him to sit. He has to have the looks *and* the skills to be successful."

Henri doesn't have to worry about either of those things. After 10 years in the business, he's as seasoned as any pro. But he's never, ever blasé about it all.

"That's such a big part of Henri's charm," says Martha. "He's so full of life that he brings a little bit more of it to everyone around him—especially me. I knew that the minute I first saw him, but I had no idea that he'd take me on such a trip!" ✪

chapter seven

A Beagle Beats the Best

*O*n a fine summer day in State College, Pennsylvania, a small, spotted beagle found herself in a contest against both man and machine.

Peaches earned her living sniffing out wood-destroying termites for her owner, Mike Del Gaudio, at his pest-control business in Scranton, Pennsylvania. Her reputation as a bug-busting miracle had spread, resulting in a challenge. At the Pennsylvania State Pest Control Convention, she would go nose-to-the-wall to beat a host of human termite inspectors and two high-tech machines.

"Peaches and I had been working together for about 2 years when I got a letter inviting us to the convention," Mike recalls. "I knew she was good, but being asked to prove it in front of all my peers was pretty scary."

Nonetheless, the pair accepted the challenge. Mike was sure that they'd beat the eyes of even the best human inspector, but he wasn't so sure about taking on technology. One machine, called the Boreoscope, was a small fiber-optic cable that could be wriggled behind walls to give the operator a bug's-eye view of the situation. The other, called Termitech, was a sensitive machine that sensed methane, a gas released by termites, in minute quantities.

Though a dog's nose can't be patented or promoted as a new invention, the old-fashioned device is a miracle that boggles the modern mind. A beagle's nose has more than 30 times as much skin devoted to scenting as does a human's. And a dog's olfactory bulb, the brain's smell center, is 4 times bigger than her master's.

Dogs also have about 200 million nerve cells that carry information from the nose to the brain; people have a meager 7 million. The sniff power of even the dullest-nosed dog is far beyond a person's ability, and perhaps beyond human imagination. But could such talent outperform an unfeeling, cold-blooded machine?

• • •

The Lone Noser

"For the demonstration, we picked a local building that we knew had termite activity," explains Robert Snetsinger, Ph.D., professor emeritus of entomology at Pennsylvania State University in University Park. "We went to the Park Forest Village Community Church, which was a beautiful older wooden building, and I checked it out carefully. I knew where we'd had recent swarms, and I knew where the termites were living."

He carefully cordoned off the church into four areas: the upper church and altar area, the basement, a furnace and storage area, and the exterior. Even though Peaches and both of the machines would be working at the same time, none would be able to see how the others were doing.

Before bringing in the dog and the two machines, Dr. Snetsinger invited all the conventioneers to make their own inspections. The entomologists and the pest-control operators all agreed on a dozen "hot spots" that the contestants should be able to detect. They then split into groups, each following a machine or Peaches, to silently observe the contestants at work.

At the signal, the two machine technicians put their tools to work immediately, but Mike entered his area alone. He wandered quietly around the upper area, planting small, flat tins under the carpeting near the altar and pews. Each tin contained a couple of live termites, a few airholes, and a little wood to keep the pests happy.

"I always put down controls to make sure that Peaches is alerting me the way she should," explains Mike. Also, since finding a termite means that Peaches gets a tasty treat from Mike, a successful sniff early in the day keeps her eager for a long day's hunt.

As Mike left the church to release the patient Peaches from her crate in the rear of his pickup truck, the skeptical conventioneers decided to have a little fun. They lifted the carpet next to the altar and snatched one of the tinned-termite controls. One pest-control operator slipped it into his pants pocket. When Mike returned with Peaches, he met with whispers, giggles, and not-too-friendly smiles.

"I was really nervous," Mike admits. "I just took a deep breath and tried not to get in her way." He knew that Peaches, who could read his emotions as clearly as she could smell bugs, might be distracted by his anxiety and refuse to work. Mustering his own enthusiasm, Mike asked, "Termites?" In answer, Peaches's body started to quiver, her head cocked, and her brown eyes glowed. "Search, search!" he cried, and the pair took off, Mike holding the dog's lead loosely as he guided her frantically sniffing nose along the walls with a wooden pointer.

Within a few minutes, Peaches lowered her nose, stopped, scratched at the carpet, and then looked eagerly up at Mike, proudly indicating that she had found termites. Since he had hidden a control in that spot, he smiled and pulled the carpet back with a flourish—only to find empty space. Peaches had hit on the stolen control.

"The guys were all laughing at me. It shook me up," Mike admits. He wasn't let in on the joke until later in the day. "I think they counted it against her, but really that was an amazing show of Peaches's ability. She didn't miss; she hit on where live termites had been only a few minutes before."

While the Boreoscope's technician was drilling small holes in the walls and feeding the tiny cable inside for a slow looksee, Peaches kept sniffing doggedly. She found several known sites, then hit avidly on a no-bug area. Mike heard snickers from the crowd once again. What they didn't know—but the dog did—was that one floor below, hidden behind concrete in the furnace area, termites ran rampant in the worst infestation in the entire building. Peaches smelled the bugs through concrete, closed doors, wood, tile, carpet, flooring—and the distraction of a site teeming with people and machines.

As the Termitech slowly and mechanically sniffed for methane, the operator regaled the crowds with sales pitches and success stories. Meanwhile, Peaches just kept finding bugs. "We hit on another couple of areas that were thought to be termite-free," says Mike. "Well, they weren't bug free. When they opened the area for visual inspection later, there were infestations of destructive carpenter ants." During her search, Peaches found not only all 12 known sites but an additional dozen as well.

At the end of the day, Steve Jacobs, senior extension associate in the department of entomology at Pennsylvania State University, tallied up the scores. "He stood up and announced that Peaches had blown the doors off everyone else," recalls Mike with a laugh. "I was amazed. She had worked perfectly, pretty much in spite of my mistakes that day."

Jacobs confirmed the findings. "Quite simply, the dog found what the machines could not," he admits.

Mike basked in the accolades for a few minutes, then slipped away to celebrate privately with his dog. "I took her to Hardee's, and she scarfed down three chili dogs," he explains a bit sheepishly. "Yeah, my vet might not have approved, but Peaches loved it."

• • •

Termites in the Blood

Even the most complex machines are rather easily manufactured. Put together a little bit of tin, a few electrodes, and a battery, and a machine is ready to work at the flip of a switch. The making of a termite-detection dog is hardly that simple. Not only must a dog learn basic obedience, but she must also graduate from an intensive insect-detection training program. And in order to succeed at termite detection, she has to have an incredible nose, a driving curiosity about what she smells, and the desire to use her skills at the whim of a human's request.

Peaches is not just a natural-born bug sniffer; she can be considered a canine prodigy. "When I first saw her, she was climbing all over a pile of lumber," says Andrew Solarz, Ph.D., co-owner of Beacon Dogs of Annapolis, Maryland, one of the few termite-dog academies in the world. "She was just a few weeks old then, very curious, and very brave." And she apparently already loved wood. Dr. Solarz closed the deal for the pup on the spot. Once Peaches was weaned, he brought her to his home for her termite education.

While Peaches was learning the ropes, Mike was getting his own education. A trained working dog costs about $10,000, but Mike found that his commitment hardly stopped with his signature on the check. "If you're going to work well with a dog, you have to build up a real relationship," he explains. "You have to know what she's thinking and how she's feeling. She has to know you, too, and want to work for you."

To keep a dog working during termite season, it takes a year-round commitment. "That's the big reason that these dogs aren't more popular today," explains Dr. Snetsinger. "They can sure find termites, but most pest-control companies don't want to put in that kind of energy and expense. They just want it easy."

Peaches thrived in the termite business. Not only would she perform up to four inspections a day with a wagging tail, but she also kept her nose working overtime just for the fun of it. "I'd be out walking her in a yard, and she'd stop at an old stump and scratch it, and get all excited about it," says Mike. "Sometimes we'd be walking down the street, and she'd veer off, practically tripping me to head toward a house. I guess she could smell termites from the road."

• • •

Life after Bugs

Because Peaches was a pet as much as she was a profit center, when Mike decided to sell his business, he elected to retire his dog rather than sell her as a company asset. "I think it was hard on her to quit. It was hard on both of us, really, but Peaches belongs with me," he explains. "We'd go out and search just for the fun of it, and we both eventually adjusted to retirement."

The new lifestyle did bring benefits. The pair moved in with Angeline Selvoski, Mike's mother, who gives them— quite literally—a taste of the good life. "When we were working, I monitored everything that Peaches ate. Food was for health and a reward for work," he explains. "But Mom is a real old-time Italian lady, and she just loves to cook. She feeds us meatballs and spaghetti and other yummy things. We've both lost our figures, no matter how hard we exercise, but Peaches is absolutely in her glory."

And, likely for the first time, the termites in the area are breathing a sigh of relief. ❂

chapter eight

An Answered Prayer in the Form of a Dog

"Go fetch!" 12-year-old Frankie Pitts called, hurling a pine stick across the grassy meadow. His two dogs—a collie mix named Murphy and a chocolate Lab named Sadie—bounded off after the prize.

Sadie was the quicker of the two. She scooped the stick into her mouth, loped back, and dropped it at Frankie's mom's feet. "She wants you to throw it this time," Frankie told her.

Tammy Pitts and her son had come to spend a sunny Saturday in February with her folks at the family's country camp near Marion, Louisiana. Together, mother and son had enjoyed a long walk through the meadow. After a few stick tosses, they circled the pond and headed back toward the cottage.

Tammy, a junior high school teacher, went inside to visit with her mother and work on the next week's lesson plans. Frankie had other ideas. He grabbed his fishing pole and headed back to the pond, both dogs following close behind.

Frankie fished from the shore for a time. Soon, though, he was frustrated by the lack of so much as a nibble. "Maybe they're all out in the middle," Frankie thought, eyeing the aluminum rowboat he and his grandfather often took out to fish the deeper water.

Frankie's grandfather was still recuperating from a recent heart operation. He was inside the cabin taking a nap. Frankie knew that there would be no fishing with his grandfather today. But Frankie was 12. "I'm old enough to handle the boat myself," he thought.

Frankie hurried to the dock and untied the lines. "Hop in," he told Sadie and Murphy. The dogs leapt into the boat, raring to go. Then, just before shoving off, Frankie did one last thing—he knotted one of the boat's tie lines around Sadie's collar. "I don't want you jumping out in the middle of the pond for a swim," he told her.

Frankie slipped the oars into the oarlocks and rowed toward deeper water. Unfortunately for Frankie, on this day, he had forgotten to replace the boat's drain plugs. Slowly, inevitably, the boat began to fill with pond water.

• • •

A Ride Gone Terribly Astray

Inside the cabin, Tammy glanced out a window just in time to spot Frankie standing ankle-deep in bilgewater. She gasped in alarm and raced outside. But by the time Tammy reached the pond, the boat had already swamped and capsized, plunging Frankie and both dogs into 14 feet of murky water.

Frankie was usually a good swimmer. But the pond was ice-cold, and every time he raised his head above water,

Murphy clambered onto his shoulders and inadvertently pushed him back under.

"Mommy!" he cried out, and went under yet again.

"I'm coming!" Tammy shouted, and dove without hesitation into the icy water. She swam with every fiber of her strength until she reached the capsized boat 40 feet from shore. She tried to push the boat toward her son so he could grab hold of it.

It wouldn't budge.

"Hurry! He's drowning!" Tammy's elderly mother, Bobbie Savage, called frantically from the shoreline. Tammy abandoned the boat and swam the rest of the way to her flailing son.

"Help me!" he gasped, grabbing his mom's shoulder and pulling her underwater with him.

"Frankie, you've got to let go so I can help you!" Tammy sputtered, struggling to free herself from her son's death grip so she could find some way to save him. But every time she fought free, Frankie grabbed her again and dragged her back under.

"Oh Frankie, I'm trying my best!" Tammy sobbed when she spotted her little boy's ashen face several inches beneath the surface. His eyes were wide open in a frantic plea for help.

Try as she might, Tammy simply could not hold her son's head above water. Her soaked sweatsuit and tennis shoes were weighing her down terribly. Her arms and legs were cramping from the cold. "We're both going to drown," Tammy realized.

When Frankie grabbed Tammy again, he pulled her onto her back. Gazing heavenward, Tammy sent up a final, desperate plea. "Dear God, please don't let us drown!"

● ● ●

An Answered Prayer

Suddenly, Tammy's head bobbed forward. She found herself staring straight into Sadie's worried brown eyes. The chocolate Lab was swimming not 5 feet away, still tethered to the boat by the tie line.

"Sadie, come here!" Tammy urged, and in just a few quick seconds, the Lab had paddled to her side with the overturned boat in tow.

Clutching Frankie's shoulder in one hand, Tammy used the other to grab Sadie's collar next to where it was attached to the tie line. "Go, Sadie, go!" she said, and instantly Sadie took off. The 65-pound Lab's powerful legs churned the water as she paddled her way toward the nearest dry land.

Tammy summoned her last ounce of strength to hold Frankie's head above water. "I hope it's not too late," she prayed.

Finally, Sadie neared the shoreline. Tammy grabbed hold of a tree root and sat in the shallow water. Exhausted, she couldn't climb the last few feet out. "Frankie? Are you okay?" she asked, clutching her son tightly in her lap.

Frankie coughed up water. "Mommy! Don't let me drown!" he sputtered weakly.

Tammy burst into great sobs of relief. "We're safe," she assured Frankie. He wrapped his numbed arms around her.

Sadie was celebrating in her own way—leaping in and out of the water, still tied to the boat she'd all but dragged ashore. Her excited barks were answered from across the pond.

"That's Murphy!" said Tammy. The frightened pound pup had also made his way safely to shore.

Tammy's mom picked her way through the thickets and helped Frankie out of the water. Tammy dragged herself out, untied Sadie, and then collapsed onto dry ground. Sadie gave herself a casual shake and plopped down beside her. Tammy buried her face in the Lab's sopping fur. "You saved us!" she told her.

A Breed Born to Swim

Tammy and Frankie may actually owe their lives to the fact that Sadie is a Labrador retriever. "As a breed, Labs are among the swiftest and most powerful swimmers," says A. Nelson Sills, president of the national Labrador Retriever Club.

Today, Labs are an extremely versatile breed. They perform duties that range from bomb sniffing to working as service animals for the blind and other disabled people. "About the only task that Labs refuse to learn is how to be attack dogs, because they just love everybody," notes Sills.

But according to Sills, the Labrador retriever was originally bred by fishermen from a coastal Canadian province for a very different job. "About 100 years ago, they crossed the Newfoundland with the black pointer," he explains. "Their goal was to breed a dog that would jump into the water and haul in the heavy fishing nets with its teeth."

Imagine the icy North Atlantic. Hundreds of pounds of fish. Man-high waves crashing all around. To Sadie, towing Frankie, his mom, and an aluminum rowboat across a small Louisiana pond must have seemed like a Sunday stroll in the park compared with the work of her forefathers.

But Sadie was a hero nonetheless. That night, after Frankie, Tammy, Murphy, and Sadie all received clean bills of health, the gentle retriever settled in to a heaping bowl of her favorite gourmet dog food.

"Frankie and I are both thankful to be alive," Tammy says. "God answered my prayers. He sent Sadie to rescue us." ✪

chapter nine

An Eye for the Hypnotic

*M*issing dogs rarely make the news. But when Hugh Lennon's black Labrador retriever, Oscar, slipped away for a few days during the Edinburgh Fringe Festival, it made headlines in this otherwise sleepy Scottish town.

"If you see this dog, don't look into his eyes!" warned the local papers. The problem wasn't that Oscar is particularly dangerous. The problem was that behind those big brown eyes is a skilled hypnotist. Gaze into his eyes for longer than 20 seconds, and you're a goner.

Skeptical? So was Hugh, a professional stage hypnotist for the past 21 years in Yorkshire, England. "A friend of mine told me that I had to go see this local farmer who claimed to have a puppy who could hypnotize people," Hugh recalls. "The instant that I saw him, I was taken with him. The dog had such unusual eyes. And he would sit and stare, completely transfixed. I bought him on the spot."

Little did Hugh know that this charming pet with the interesting eyes would become a show stealer. "I decided to take him onstage with me one night, just to see what would happen," he says. "He was a huge success. All these people were just kneeling before him, staring into his eyes, and ending up in a heap on the floor—completely hypnotized—in a matter of moments. That was 9 years ago. Now he's the main attraction: Oscar, the Amazing HypnoDog."

• • •

The Powers of Persuasion

So how do everyday, intelligent folks fall under the spell of a dog? "It really is all in the mind," says Hugh. "Hypnotism works by staring at someone long enough that the left side of his brain—the half responsible for conscious reasoning—'switches off.' What remains is the right, or subconscious, side, which is all imagination. That's why people are so susceptible to suggestions while they're under hypnosis."

Hugh freely admits that not everyone is hypnotizable. "If a person is receptive and relaxed, he collapses on the floor within a matter of seconds. Other people take longer to go under. And some don't go at all. But that's hypnotism in general, not just Oscar. If someone is hypnotizable, Oscar can put him under. I even turn my back so people don't think that I'm the one they're looking at."

Once they're under, it's anything goes. Though Hugh would never do anything to put his audience members in jeopardy, he does like to have some good-natured fun. After all, that's what the show is all about, he says.

"We mainly do comedy. I may have a group of young ladies convinced that they're the Spice Girls; they'll sing a number for us," he says.

That's the real intrigue of the show, Hugh adds. It's not just one person on stage with the dog. He'll line up a dozen or so volunteers from the audience, have them kneel down to Oscar's level, and ask them to stare into the Lab's eyes as he makes his way down the line.

Then, one by one, the willing accomplices will be out cold on the floor waiting for Hugh's next outrageous suggestion, whether it's to prance about the stage like Madonna or to order the audience to attention like an army drill sergeant.

But the best show memories are those that are made after Oscar goes offstage and starts wandering through the auditorium, says Hugh. "My favorite incident happened one night when Oscar went wandering out into the crowd looking, as usual, for some food. He came across this chap eating potato crisps. Being a dog, of course, he sat right in front of him and

stared intently while the fellow crunched away," he says. "Before you knew it, there was a roar of excitement and commotion. The man had become fixed by his stare and fallen off his chair, totally hypnotized!"

Oscar, meanwhile, helped himself to a few chips.

* * *

Tools of the Trade

Having never seen the show personally, it's impossible to say how much of the hypnotizing the dog is actually doing, says Myrna M. Milani, D.V.M., an animal behaviorist in Charlestown, New Hampshire, and author of *DogSmart* and *CatSmart*. "But it's not out of the realm of possibility that this dog can put people into an altered mental state," she says. "We know that dogs have a powerful calming effect on people. That could certainly be part of what happens during these shows."

Because dogs have been bred to hunt, herd, and track, they also are able to reach a deep state of concentration, says Dr. Milani. "Certain dogs can hold a steady gaze on a point of interest for a long time. And it sounds like this dog is certainly one of those."

Combine all these innate canine traits with the persuasive powers of a trained hypnotist, and you might be on to something, she says. "Someone who is well-trained in the skills of hypnotism can put people under using anything from a pocket watch to a pendulum. If the dog is able to sit very still and hold a steady gaze, that would work, too. And when you think about it, wouldn't you rather stare into a dog's eyes than at a pocket watch?"

Of course, none of this works on everybody, says Dr. Milani. "There are certain people who seem to have a positive predisposition to being hypnotized. If you're one of them, I don't see why a dog couldn't do the job. If you aren't, then he won't."

• • •

Coming Soon to a Theatre near You

Still dubious? You may be able to see Oscar's amazing antics firsthand someday soon. Oscar has received countless invitations from the likes of David Letterman and other American entertainers.

But until recently, he has had to turn them down, because United Kingdom quarantine laws mandate that dogs returning from trips abroad must be quarantined for 6 months, Hugh says. "I simply could never do that to Oscar. I don't care how big the show is."

Fortunately, now that vaccination is becoming routine in the United States and Canada, those laws are being revisited. Before long, Hugh hopes to be able to acquire a pet passport and take Oscar's show to the States.

Just remember, look too long, and *you* may become part of this most unusual act. ☻

chapter ten

False Pregnancy, Real Love

*F*ighting like cats and dogs: It's an expression we've all heard and used. That's how ingrained the image of a bristly tailed feline treed by a barking dog is in our culture.

Even many a veterinarian has separate waiting rooms marked "for dogs" and "for cats." If there's one thing we've learned from Saturday-morning cartoons while growing up, it's this: cats and dogs are mortal enemies.

But every once in a while, some dogs forget that, when they spot a member of the opposite species, they're supposed to extinguish one or two of its nine lives. That's what happened when Rizzie, a German shepherd–Shetland sheepdog mix, suddenly found herself sharing a house with a litter of rescued kittens.

● ● ●

Rizzie Comes In from the Cold

In days past, no matter what the weather in Warminster, Pennsylvania, Rizzie could be found outside braving it. She spent much of her time nosing through trash cans for old cantaloupe rinds and scraps of meat. The rest of the time, she sought shelter from wind, rain, or snow under awnings and bushes. Rizzie did have an owner, but the owner was dealing with problems of her own and had little time to care for her dog.

Stephanie Halczenko, who lived next door to Rizzie's owner, often found the black, tan, and white dog huddling under her window to escape the rain. In fact, Steph noticed, Rizzie visited so often that the dog eventually wore a permanent path through the hedges dividing their yards.

"Rizzie was left outside to run around and fend for herself. To me, that's not what a dog should have to live with," says Steph. "She used to come by covered with ticks—we'd pick 20 to 30 off of her at one time."

Rizzie came to depend on Steph for baths, food, and attention. Because Steph knew that her parents, with whom she lived, wouldn't want her to become attached to Rizzie, she didn't call the dog over too often. But she did frequently call her own cats, knowing that the dog would appear like magic at the sound of her voice.

This arrangement went on for 2 years. Then, the winter of 1995 ushered in unusually stormy weather and subzero temperatures. Rizzie hid on Steph's doorstep.

"One day, I called her over, and her teeth were chattering," says Steph. "My father asked why she was doing that, and I said that it was because she was freezing." Rizzie became a member of the Halczenko family that day.

● ● ●

New Kits on the Block

In September of 1997, a distraught woman rushed three mewling kittens into the veterinary hospital where Steph worked. The 3-week-old kittens were crawling with fleas and so dirty that Steph couldn't tell where the dirt stopped and the kittens' natural coloring began.

The local woman had seen a man about to drown the litter in a river in the Pocono mountains, and she had offered to take the kittens instead. She knew that any home she could find for them would be better than the fate that presently stared them in the face.

The kittens were so young that they hadn't even been weaned. Just like newborn babies, they required constant attention and care. Steph bundled the litter into her home and dutifully fed them every 3 hours, day and night.

Steph thought nothing of it when Rizzie watched intently while she cleaned the kittens and when Rizzie whined softly every time they cried. She attributed it to jealousy. Rizzie had become used to being the baby in the family, after all, and now she was expected to share the house with an entire litter of an enemy species.

But, for Rizzie, jealousy was never a factor. She had dropped her canine defenses and forgotten the age-old stereotype that cats and dogs are natural foes. A few days after the litter came home with Steph, Rizzie was cuddling the kittens, gently herding them around the house and letting them doze against her fur.

• • •

Feline Foster Care

Steph, seeing that Rizzie wanted to play a part in the kittens' care, eventually let the dog take over cleaning duty. She had only to command, "Clean them up," and Rizzie would go into grooming mode, gently licking the kittens' ruffled fur and nibbling away the tangles.

Rizzie also made room for the kittens at her food bowl whenever they decided to sneak a taste of her dog chow. She even taught them to play with her toys and dog bones.

"She played with them like she would have played with puppies," Steph recalls. "They'd curl up next to her, and she'd kind of mouth them, and they'd swat at her head." In fact, the only thing Rizzie didn't let the kittens do was nurse. When they tried, she'd simply get up and move away, grumbling softly in the way that mother dogs issue warnings to their pups.

What becomes of kittens that are raised by their "natural enemy"? Cats are amazingly adaptable creatures. So much so that, when they're raised by a dog, they tend to act like dogs. Rizzie's kittens have grown up to be as playful and sociable as puppies—and they live a life filled with dog bones, kibble, and tail-chasing games.

• • •

Make-Believe Mother

Steph attributes Rizzie's maternal nature to the fact that she probably never had puppies of her own. The unspayed Rizzie was experiencing false pregnancy when Steph brought her home, meaning that her body was going through the physical changes of pregnancy even though she was not actually pregnant.

According to Mary Lee Nitschke, Ph.D., an animal-behavior therapist and associate professor of psychology at Linfield College Portland Campus in Oregon, "False pregnancy is not rare in dogs. And if a dog is rewarded for its experience, as Rizzie was when she was adopted, then it builds a 'behavior chain.' The chemicals that cause false pregnancy wear off, but the maternal instinct is maintained by the experiences that the dog had during that time."

Rizzie may also have picked up her warmhearted nature and love for all animals from her owner. Steph has volunteered as an animal rescue worker and worked for a vet for years. She also fosters orphaned animals and is a member of Animal Orphans and Save a Shepherd Rescue Alliance, an organization that takes in abandoned dogs and finds them homes.

Steph's work with young animals may have played the biggest role in igniting Rizzie's maternal instincts. "If dogs are around young of another species toward which the owner displays protective behavior, in general, the dogs will also be protective," Dr. Nitschke explains.

So, the question remains: Were the Saturday-morning cartoons right? Are cats and dogs really sworn enemies? If Rizzie is any example, the answer is no. Sometimes stereotypes need to be broken—and Rizzie was just the dog to do it. ✪

chapter eleven

Duane and Goliath

*O*n a good day, Duane Wright noodles around on his home computer for an hour or so, designing posters for the school where his wife, Arlene, works as a secretary. Sometimes he whiles away a quiet afternoon watching a ball game on television.

All too often, though, Duane can manage nothing more strenuous than sitting quietly in his chair, struggling to catch his breath. But no matter what he's doing, no matter how poorly he feels, one thing is for sure: Duane's pet iguana, Goliath, is never too far from his side.

For years, Duane wished that he could have a pet, something warm and cuddly to keep him company. Unfortunately, Duane lives with a multitude of serious respiratory disorders, including valley fever (a fungal infection of the lungs), chronic asthma, and severe sleep apnea.

He lives in a world of air purifiers, respirators, and oxygen tanks. He spends most of every day confined to a temperature- and humidity-controlled room in his Tucson, Arizona, home. A pet might have made the isolation a bit more bearable for Duane, but doctors warned him that adopting a dog, a cat, or even a bird could jeopardize his already precarious health.

"They told me that breathing in the dander, fur, or feathers could kill me," recalls the former office equipment serviceman.

And then several Christmases ago, Duane's teenage son, Duane Jr., had an idea. He skipped lunches at school and saved his money. On Christmas morning, his dad was delighted to discover a 10-gallon aquarium containing a baby iguana waiting for him underneath the tree.

Lizards are not warm-blooded, but some of them sure are warmhearted. Goliath showed her cuddly side quickly. With no fur or feathers to aggravate Duane's breathing problems, man and iguana became fast friends. Duane enjoyed taking his pet lizard out of her tank and stroking her spiny back until, in-

variably, she dozed off in his arms. Every night, he let her wriggle contentedly beneath his pillow or sleep stretched full-length across his chest.

• • •

An Inseparable Pair

In time, the now 3-foot-long, 7-pound reptile became rather attached to Duane, to say the least.

"Most evenings, I visit Duane in his room and sit watching TV with him for a while," describes Arlene. "But whenever I try to hold my husband's hand, Goliath stares at me with her eyes narrowed into slits, and if I don't let go, she starts spitting at me."

"Much like dogs and cats, iguanas often become active participants in family life," says Dolly Ellerbrock, cofounder of the Pittsburgh Herpetological Society and author of *Your Easy Guide to Care, Training, and Breeding of Common Green Iguanas.* (Herpetology is the study of reptiles.)

"They do usually tend to develop an extra close bond with one particular family member—usually the person who takes care of the feeding," she adds. According to Ellerbrock, it's not at all uncommon for a pet iguana to demonstrate clear signs of jealousy when it comes to a caretaker. "Iguanas can be very possessive," she explains.

• • •

Jealousy Rears Its Pretty Head

That may be exactly what happened one night when Goliath was hunkered down in her "cave," an overturned wooden crate covered in grass carpeting. "She wouldn't come out, no matter how much I coaxed her," Duane recalls. "But then Arlene came into the room. She sat down on the hospital bed beside me.

You should have seen that little lady come flying out of her crate and wriggle between us."

On another night, about a year ago, Duane tried several times to get Goliath to stay in her cave. "I was feeling especially weak that night. I was having even more trouble than usual getting my breath, and I really didn't want her sleeping on top of me." But Goliath refused to sleep anywhere else and, as it happened, that turned out to be a fortunate thing indeed.

"We have an intercom connecting our bedrooms," says Arlene. "Sometime around 1:00 A.M., I was awakened by a strange commotion coming from Duane's room. I climbed out of bed and hurried to see what was the matter. But when I opened Duane's door and switched on the light, I could hardly believe my eyes."

There was Goliath, perched on Duane's chest, smacking him soundly in the face with her tail and nipping him repeatedly on the cheek. Goliath kept making loud sneezing noises through her nostrils, and she was scratching her unconscious friend on the chest so vigorously that she actually drew blood.

Arlene knew immediately what was wrong. "Duane had stopped breathing," she recalls with a shudder. Arlene rushed to Duane's aid, and between lizard and lady they managed to connect the respirator and restart Duane's lungs just in time. Arlene then summoned an ambulance, which raced Duane to the hospital for emergency medical care.

"I don't know how she did it, but Goliath must have sensed what was wrong," says a grateful Duane. "Were it not for all the commotion Goliath raised, Arlene would have slept right through, and I never would have survived the night. As strange as it may sound, I owe my life to Goliath."

No Surprise to Iguanas

"Iguanas are very misunderstood creatures," observes Eller-brock. "Many people are frightened by them, but if you take the time to look an iguana in the eyes and give him lots of touch and affection, he'll almost always return your love many times over." Indeed, Ellerbrock has known of several iguanas who were so devoted to their caretakers that when fate stepped in and separated them, the lonely reptiles simply shut down and died.

So how did Goliath know that Duane was in critical respiratory distress? "Sleeping stretched out on Duane like that, she may have sensed that his chest had stopped rising and falling," Ellerbrock speculates. Of course, this doesn't explain why Goliath went to such lengths to try to save Duane's life. Nor does it explain a similar incident that happened to Ellerbrock herself.

"My husband, Herb, was sleeping in his easy chair, snoring fairly loudly," she recalls. "Suddenly, he stopped snoring, and in a flash our 16-year-old iguana, Charlie, had leapt off the couch beside me and climbed into Herb's lap. Charlie stuck her nose right into Herb's face, and she kept snorting at him until finally he woke up."

These days, Duane's green guardian angel takes up sentry duty on his chest every night. "She's wakened me many times with her tail and teeth since that first time, and whenever she does, I always feel so weak that I know I must have stopped breathing again. It's reached the point where I'm afraid to go to sleep without Goliath sleeping right here on my chest," he says.

"I know I certainly breathe easier knowing that Goliath is on the job," adds Arlene. ✪

chapter twelve

Ryan's Incredible Journey

The days were numbered for the Irish setter named Ryan. For many months, he'd been passed from family to family. But still, Ryan had no home. He was a sweet and gentle animal who loved children. An ideal family pet, except for one problem.

Ryan hated being left by himself. Home alone, he would invariably vent his displeasure by chewing up the furniture and rugs and forgetting his house training.

When Ryan wound up at a Sacramento, California, pound, members of the Irish Setter Club of America's local rescue league stepped in and placed him in doggie foster care until a good home could be found. But first they took him to the vet for a checkup.

That night, a security guard was startled to discover Ryan staring at him through the reception-office window. The lonesome pooch had escaped from his kennel and chewed his way through a back-room doorjamb. "Please don't leave me here alone," Ryan's sad brown eyes seemed to cry out.

Rescue league members Paul Armbruster and Marilee Larson placed Ryan in several different homes, but he was always back in less than a week. "We may have to put him down," Paul said sadly one day, after they took Ryan to an animal fair. No one had stepped forward to offer him a home.

But Ryan had one last hope. A few months earlier, John and Vicky Pierson had contacted the rescue league hoping to adopt an Irish setter puppy. Ryan was no pup, but Marilee figured that it couldn't hurt to ask the Piersons whether they'd consider adopting an older setter.

The Piersons agreed to try Ryan in their home for a month, despite his problematic history. The couple had six children, so there was little chance that Ryan would ever be left home alone. "He seems like a great dog," John said when Paul introduced the family to their new pet. "He reminds me of an Irish setter we used to have, named Randy."

● ● ●

From Country to City Living and Back

For many years, the Piersons had lived in a rural California mountain community named Spring Valley. The family loved country life, but the nearest school was an hour's bus ride over the mountains. As the family grew ever larger, there seemed to be little choice. "We have to move closer to town," John decided.

At the time, the family owned a pair of Irish setters named Randy and Angel. Unfortunately, their new landlord would permit them to have only one. "It's the only house we can afford that's big enough for our family," John told his wife. "We'll have to find a new home for Randy, because Angel is too old. No one would adopt her."

A few weeks later, the whole family waved a sad goodbye as Randy rode off with his new owner to a farm in Reno, Nevada. "At least he has a good home," John and the others comforted themselves whenever they thought about their lost friend.

Now, 2½ years later, the Piersons were moving into a different, larger house, in the town of Clear Lake. They couldn't wait to adopt another Irish setter to help fill the emptiness that still ached in their hearts.

"I hope Ryan makes the best of his very last chance," Paul told Marilee as they drove away from the Piersons' house. Back at his own home, the moment that Paul walked in the door, the telephone began to ring. It was John.

"We love Ryan already! We want to keep him. Send us the adoption papers right away!"

Paul was delighted that Ryan seemed to be fitting in so well, but he knew from experience that the setter's problems didn't always show up right away. "Let's wait a few weeks and then see if you still feel the same," he advised cautiously.

● ● ●

Ryan Finds a Home

The first night in his new home, Ryan walked up to the family cat, Tigem, and rubbed noses. Later, he wandered from bedroom to bedroom looking in on the sleeping children.

"These are the same things that Randy used to do," John observed as Ryan curled up on a living-room rug with 13-year-old Angel.

Ryan adjusted quickly to his new home and family. He spent countless happy hours chasing a ball with the kids and swimming with them in a nearby pond. One day, John took the whole family to Six Flags Marine World. He felt nervous about leaving Ryan unsupervised, but that night when the family returned home, they found him snoozing contentedly on the living-room floor with the cat.

The Piersons loved their new friend. Still, it puzzled them that he reminded them so much of their old friend, Randy. "He sits with his rear end on the couch and his feet on the floor just like Randy used to do," John told Paul one night on the phone. "And whenever he wants something, instead of barking, he sort of talks quietly to us."

"Those are common Irish setter behaviors," Paul told John.

"You're right, of course," John agreed. "It's just that we all still miss Randy so much."

And then, one day, the family visited a park in Spring Valley where Randy used to play. When it was time to leave, Ryan headed toward home—only it wasn't toward his new home in Clear Lake but, rather, toward the Piersons' old home in Spring Valley, where Randy had lived as a pup.

"It has to be Randy come back to us!" John marveled. "There's simply no other explanation!"

During Ryan's next vet visit, John mentioned the many coincidences and the family's suspicions. "It would be easy enough to find out," said the vet. "Remember several years ago when Randy got a foxtail caught in his paw and I had to remove it surgically? If this is Randy, there should be a scar."

The vet clipped away a bit of Ryan's fur. Sure enough, the old scar was clearly visible. Ryan was really Randy, and after 2½ years he was finally back home with the people he loved.

A Memory for Love

"We love dogs because they love us unconditionally," observes Jeffrey Moussaieff Masson, author of *Dogs Never Lie about Love*. "A dog's capacity for love is so pronounced, so developed, that it's almost like another sense or another organ. It might well be called hyperlove."

According to Masson, dogs who are separated from their loved ones will often become listless and depressed. Some, like Randy, may even develop behavior problems. "Perhaps that's why Ryan could not stand to be left alone," Masson speculates. "The solitude may have reminded him too much of the pain of missing his real family and home."

But now Randy is home, and even if it did take the Piersons some time to realize this, apparently, Randy knew it from the very first night when he rubbed noses with the cat and looked in on all the kids. "Dogs have a prodigious memory for people they have known," says Masson. "When a dog loves you, he loves you always, no matter what you do, no matter how much time goes by."

Was it fate that led Randy back home, or merely coincidence? To the Piersons, it couldn't matter less. "What really counts is that he is back," says John. "And now that he's home, we'll never let him go again." ✪

chapter thirteen

A Nose for Bees

When frost settles softly on Maryland's fields and farms, it's a sure signal that winter's chill is not far away. Most dogs— even housebound ones who plan to keep snug by the fire— begin to grow thick, warm coats and layers of fat in hopes of hunkering down when snow and sleet fill the air.

But for one yellow Labrador retriever, a nose-nipping frost brings sparkling eyes and a wagging tail. For him, wintertime is pure fun. It's the season when he puts his nose to work.

Bynoe is a dog with a unique mission: He sniffs out sick honeybees. He's an employee of the Maryland Department of Agriculture, and his sensitive nose has been put to work as a powerful weapon in the war against American foulbrood, a deadly honeybee disease.

A bacterial infection, foulbrood attacks honeybee larvae (the brood) and quickly turns them into a foul mass of decay. As the hive sickens, bees from other hives invade, rob the infected honey, and carry it back to their own broods, spreading the disease.

From only one infected colony, foulbrood can kill more than 50 percent of the colonies within a beeyard in just 1 year, and it can spread up to 3 miles in that same time. "If we didn't control this disease, it would be devastating," says Bart Smith, supervisor of the apiary inspection program for the Maryland Department of Agriculture.

But Bynoe has no plans to let the disease slip by his sensitive nose. "This is one dog who loves to work," says Jerry Fischer, state apiary inspector and Bynoe's two-legged partner. "And he's incredibly good at it. He can inspect 200 hives in 20 minutes. Of course, since the hives are spread out, we spend most of the day driving." Typically, Jerry and Bynoe inspect about 14 beeyards of 60 to 65 colonies each in a day.

When humans hunt foulbrood, it's much slower going. "When a person inspects a hive, he has to open it up and take a good look around. It takes time. A single inspector can look at maybe 30 hives in a good day," says Smith.

People are the prime bee-disease hunters in the summertime, primarily because they also need to check on less deadly diseases, such as tracheal mites, which Bynoe has not been trained to smell. Hibernating hives can't be opened in cold weather, though, because it could damage the bees, so winter inspections are strictly a dog's game. "He keeps us working year-round," says Smith.

● ● ●

At Home with Hives

On a typical day, Bynoe takes a light breakfast, then leaps into Jerry's truck. The two may head to the shores of the Chesapeake Bay or west toward the snowy mountains. Whatever the scenery, the ultimate destination is a sleeping beeyard. Bynoe eagerly awaits his cue, then sniffs each hive with his tail wagging and a bounce in his step.

If there's foulbrood inside a hive, Bynoe sits beside it, looks at his partner, and vibrates with excitement. Jerry praises him, and they celebrate with a game of ball on the outskirts of the beeyard. Then, Jerry marks the hive so the disease can be confirmed and the hive can be decontaminated during the first warm days of spring, before the bees begin to fly.

Maryland isn't the only state with a foulbrood problem—the disease attacks bees nationwide—but it is the only state to call in the dog. Maryland officials trained the very first bee dog known, a Labrador named Max. He began work in 1985 to help a three-man human inspection team. Although several other states tried to train foulbrood-sniffing dogs, by 1991, when Bynoe had been trained to fill Max's aging pawprints, there were no other bee dogs left working in the United States. Or anywhere else in the world. Too few dogs, it turned out, had the ability to sniff out the disease accurately.

The Importance of Bees

To many folks, the mild-mannered honeybee is at best a curiosity, at worst a flying fear factory. In fact, bees are vital to our existence. "People just don't realize how important bees are to them personally," says Commander Loyd Luna, a retired naval officer and apiary educator who lives in Arnold, Maryland. And it's not just the honey that's important, it's the pollination work that bees do. "We say that 33 percent of everything that shows up on your table has to be pollinated by a honeybee," explains Jerry. "Think about it—that's a lot of food."

The Maryland Department of Agriculture estimates that the state's 1,000 beekeepers produce a honey crop valued at $6 billion a year. The pollination value tops $20 billion a year. And that still doesn't measure all the value packed into a honeybee. "It's not just commercial crops they pollinate," says Commander Luna. "It's also the wildflowers that feed butterflies. And the plants and trees that provide forage for all of the birds and wild animals, too." Without the buzz of honeybees, life would be very different and nowhere near as sweet.

• • •

The Making of a Bee Dog

Ten years ago, a bouncing baby Labrador was born in Baltimore. By weaning time, he'd been adopted by a local teenager, who named him after Bono, the energetic lead singer in the popular rock group U2. With his name spelled phonetically in a Baltimore accent, "Bynoe" was donated to the Baltimore County K-9 Corps when he was just 11 months old.

"The boy who donated him said he just couldn't keep him at home anymore, I guess because he had so much energy," says Rick Johnston, senior trainer for the Corps. "I need smart, high-energy dogs, so he worked out well here."

Training a dog to sniff foulbrood is not a lot different from teaching it to detect drugs or explosives, says Johnston. The bottom line for all detection work lies in a dog's supersensitive sense of smell, which is said to be up to a million times more sensitive than a person's.

"Just imagine how much you can smell with your own nose," says Johnston, "then try to think what it would be like to smell even a thousand times better. How amazing that would be. What smells offensive to you would be really nasty to a dog's nose."

Johnston is one of the few people who have actually smelled foulbrood, which is normally considered odorless to humans. "I got it very, very concentrated in a small can and then let it get nice and warm in the sun," he explains. "When I opened that can, I could catch a whiff. Boy, did it smell awful."

Bynoe, on the other hand, can stand 150 feet away and smell even the smallest infection in a hive stacked behind a dozen others. Of course, since there are often 100 hives packed into a quarter-acre lot, long-distance sniffing is not encouraged. "We taught Bynoe to work within an inch of the hives," says Jerry. "He might know which hive is infected from 5 feet away, but I won't know until he tells me."

The secret to Bynoe's training is a four-letter word: ball. "This dog is crazy about balls, so we hid one inside empty hives along with a little American foulbrood," says Johnston. "When he found his ball, we played a game of fetch and had a great time. He had no idea he was looking for disease; he thought that he was hunting out his ball." In just a few short sessions, Bynoe learned that sitting next to a hive that smelled like his foulbrood-scented ball meant playtime, and he couldn't wait to go to work.

Training did bring a few painful moments. "We tried working in warm weather when the bees were flying, and sometimes we'd get stung," says Johnston. "I didn't like being stung, and neither did the dog. He'd try to wipe the bees off his nose with a paw, and then he'd back off a little. He never quit, but they were a distraction. We quickly learned that the best time to work a dog is when the bees are hibernating. No distractions."

Once Bynoe's nose was trained to the scent, he became a virtually perfect sniffing machine. To prove his nasal prowess, he is put to a formal test every 3 months. A score of less than 98 percent would sideline him until his nose could be retuned with formal K-9 training. In his 8 years of service, Bynoe has simply never missed a hive.

"I really can't take credit for that kind of performance," says Johnston. "What makes or breaks the dog is the bond between the dog and the handler. I watched Jerry and Bynoe form a big bond. Each always seemed to know exactly what the other was thinking. Bynoe loves his ball, but it's obvious that his real reward is just hearing Jerry say, 'Good dog!'"

● ● ●

Not Just a Dumb Dog

"Boy, I hate it when I hear someone say, 'Aw, they're just dumb dogs,'" says Jerry. "There's nothing dumb about a dog, especially this one. Once you get a highly trained, intelligent dog like this, you find out that they are so smart that they almost scare you. This dog can read me like a book, and he's very aware of my every move. I can have a casual conversation with someone and tell them where we're going and what vehicle I'm planning to use, and when we head outside, he'll go

74

straight to the right car. Some people think that you can tie a dog to a tree and feed him once a day, then expect him to use his intelligence to help you work. You just can't do that."

Bynoe has never seen the long end of a rope. Instead, he lounges on his bed and cruises the kitchen of Jerry's house, just like one of the family. He even dotes on an assortment of stuffed animals. "He's always carrying one around," explains Jerry. "He can't even go out for a walk without one in his mouth. When I grab the leash, he heads for the toy box and picks one out."

Bynoe takes perfect care of his pets, tucking them back into the toy box each night at bedtime but saving one to sleep with. His favorite companion is a tiny stuffed bear that Jerry gave him as a welcome present when he moved in almost 9 years ago. Bynoe carries it around outdoors like a prize, but he won't drop it on the ground, even if he has to greet strangers with a bear-muffled bark.

Although the Maryland Department of Agriculture officially owns Bynoe, it has no plans to break up the team. "Well, I guess he's pretty much Jerry's pet," says Smith. "When he retires, he'll just live a life of ease right at home where he belongs."

"Retirement?" says Jerry, pausing to consider the implications for the aging 10-year-old Lab. "Surely he's got another good 2 years or more in him."

Another pause, and Jerry continues. "You know, I've been doing this a long time myself. When we first started, we used to jump out of the truck and run full speed to the yards, and jump over the fences in our way. Now, I park closer and we walk. We're both slowing down. But he'd hate being retired. For him, work is a game that he loves."

And if Jerry has his way, what Bynoe loves is what Bynoe gets. ✪

chapter fourteen

A Part of One Saves Two

*T*he abandoned kitten lay curled up in a cage at the SPCA in Buffalo. He had thought that he had found a home, but the woman who had adopted him had had to bring him back. "My husband is allergic," she explained, handing the kitten to a volunteer at the shelter.

"Sorry, little fella," the volunteer had sighed, returning the kitten to the cage with all of the others. There were so many abandoned animals and so few people willing to give them homes—it wasn't likely that this kitten would get a second chance.

At the same time, 450 miles away in Richmond, Virginia, Sandy Carr clutched her cat to her breast. "I'm sorry. Smokey has irreversible, progressive kidney disease," the vet grimly told her. "The only thing that we can do is try to keep him as comfortable as possible."

The future looked bleak for both of these cats. But that was before fate stepped in and brought them together in a very special way that would allow the two to save each other's life.

Like the kitten in Buffalo, Smokey began his life as an unwanted stray. Only, Smokey never made it to a shelter. Instead, he and a dozen other feral cats eked out a marginal existence near Sandy and Peyton Carr's Chesapeake Bay vacation cottage.

Sandy's heart went out to the scraggly, malnourished ragamuffins. During their frequent weekends at the bay, she and her husband always made sure to bring along plenty of cat food. When some of the animals grew sick, the couple spent several days rounding up the lot and carrying them to the vet for their shots and for spaying and neutering.

Then, the Carrs released the animals back into the wild. The cats were grateful that at last someone cared about them. They always came running whenever the Carrs pulled into their cottage's driveway.

On Sunday evenings, when it was time for Sandy and Peyton to head home, the cats gathered on the cottage porch to watch them pack the car. Sandy could almost hear each cat pleading, "Take me with you. Please?"

One by one, that was exactly what Sandy and Peyton did. Eventually, the couple wound up adopting an even dozen of the strays—including the gray-and-white tom with tuxedo markings whom they named Smokey.

* * *

A Newly Found Family

For the Carrs, the cats became the children they never had. Each cat found a special place in their hearts and in their home. The couple always made sure that their feline family had plenty of nutritious food on hand and saw to it that each received the best veterinary care available.

And so one day, when Sandy noticed a faint whiff of ammonia on Smokey's breath, she loaded him into a kennel carrier and carried him to the vet's office. She fought back tears as the doctor described Smokey's condition. "His kidneys are failing. He's relatively healthy for now, but it's only a matter of time. There is no cure."

"What about dialysis or a kidney transplant?" Sandy inquired. She knew that these things were possible because she'd read about them in her cat magazine.

"It's something that we can look into, I suppose," replied the vet, but Sandy sensed that he wasn't enthused by the prospect. Still, Sandy was determined to give Smokey every chance at life.

That night, Peyton logged on to the Internet. "Does anyone know anything about kidney transplants for cats?" he typed in a feline-health message area. Almost immediately, several fellow cat-loving Internet users responded with names and phone numbers. The closest feline kidney specialist, Ross Lirtzman, D.V.M., had recently established a practice in Buffalo. Sandy telephoned him the very next morning.

"I think that I can help," Dr. Lirtzman replied after Sandy had described Smokey's condition.

Sandy was thrilled by the news, but she was also taken aback when Dr. Lirtzman advised her that the operation might cost several thousand dollars.

That night, Sandy and Peyton discussed the matter at length and decided to dip into their savings for the transplant. "It always hurts so much when a pet gets sick and there's nothing that you can do to help," says Sandy. "Peyton and I couldn't imagine how badly we would have felt if Smokey had died and there had been something more that we could have done."

Tests determined that Smokey was free from other diseases that might have jeopardized the transplant. But Dr. Lirtzman still had one concern. He explained that during the past 12 months, the Buffalo SPCA had taken in more than 6,000 cats, and almost two-thirds of them had needed to be euthanized for lack of good homes. "I can look for a donor cat at the shelter," he offered. "But only with the condition that when this is over, you'll adopt the donor cat and give it a good home."

"Of course!" Sandy agreed immediately. There was always room in her heart for another cat—especially any cat who saved her beloved Smokey's life.

• • •

Finding Buffalo in Buffalo

Peyton drove Smokey to Buffalo for the operation. Meanwhile, Dr. Lirtzman drew blood from two sheltered kittens and tested them for compatibility. They both matched.

Sandy was at a loss. "How can I pick which cat will live and which cat will probably be put to death?" she anguished.

But that was before Peyton called from the shelter to report. "One of the possible donor cats is black and white. The other is buff colored," he said.

Sandy gasped in surprise. She had already decided to name the donor kitten Buffalo in honor of the city where Smokey's life would be saved. "Pick the buff-colored kitten," she said, sensing, somehow, that this was a sign meant to relieve her of the burden of the decision.

In a 4½-hour operation, Dr. Lirtzman removed a kidney the size of a small plum from Buffalo and transplanted it into Smokey. Two days later, the donor cat was well enough to travel with Peyton to Virginia to meet the rest of his new adoptive family. And by the middle of the following week, Dr.

Lirtzman could be found sitting on his clinic floor playing with his favorite patient.

Three weeks after Smokey's transplant, Sandy flew to Buffalo to collect her furry friend. His kidney failure was a thing of the past, and today, Smokey is still doing fine. He and Buffalo are best buddies. They love chasing one another around the house or racing up and down the stairs.

"Better than 80 percent of feline kidney transplants are successful," states Lynda Bernsteen, D.V.M., a small-animal surgical resident at the University of California, Davis, Veterinary Medical Teaching Hospital. "I know of one cat who's still going strong nearly 10 years after receiving a new kidney."

The very first feline kidney transplant was performed at the university in 1986. Currently, nearly 20 veterinary centers across the United States perform the life-saving surgery.

Many of the surgical techniques and antirejection medications used in Smokey's transplant were originally developed for human kidney patients, which suits Sandy just fine. "After all, you hear about animals being used for medical research to benefit humans; it's wonderful to know that medical techniques developed to save people can be used to save not just one cat's life, but two." ❂

chapter fifteen

A Four-Legged Golf Cart

*H*ere's a riddle for you: What has four legs, three letters in its name, and has been called man's best friend?

Nope, not dog (although this other four-legged, three-lettered creature is equally affectionate and just about as smart). Think more independent. Loves playing with kids, but as soon as it gets bored will wander off.

Cat? Not even close. This baby has a bigger, noisier personality (and can grow up to weigh nearly 400 pounds). Here's a hint: This is no common companion (there are maybe 10,000 in the world today).

Stumped? Okay, it's an ass. But nobody is talking about your run-of-the-mill, ordinary variety of *Equus asinus* here. That's because there's nothing ordinary about Winston, Barbara Taylor's friend, pet, and—once in a while—golf cart.

Derived from the Latin, *Equus asinus* is the scientific name for a species whose breeds include the ass, or donkey, and the burro. As the *Equus* part of the term would indicate, horses (*Equus caballus*) and asses are similar—yet separate—species with the ability to interbreed (the offspring are known as mules).

But unlike the muttlike mule or the standard burro, which ranges in size from just over 36 inches to 48 inches in height, Winston and the other stock that Barbara raises on her ranch in Maitland, Ontario, Canada, are both pure of blood and small. They never reach more than 36 inches in height.

● ● ●

A Fascinating History

Winston and his siblings are a breed apart, dating back more than 2,000 years to the lands in and around the Mediterranean

Sea. These unique asses are better known as miniature Sicilian donkeys . . . Sicilians, for short.

Because of their surefooted sturdiness, Sicilians often hauled local crops such as grapes up and down the rough, tough terrain of their native country. And because of their low-slung power, Sicilians were also used to lug equipment and rocks through the tight shafts of southern Italian mines.

Barbara, who began raising miniature donkeys about 10 years ago, compares them favorably to their more renowned equine cousins. "Sicilians are brighter than horses. They catch on faster. I think that they're also more patient than horses. For example, if you put something on their backs for the first time, they'll accept it. Whereas, if you put something on a horse's back for the first time, he'll do everything to try to get rid of it."

What accounts for the Sicilians' margin of smarts and maturity?

Barbara surmises that it's because they have an extra month's gestation. "A horse has 11 months, a donkey has 12 months. So, when Sicilians are born, they're much more complete. They're up immediately and ready to go. Their legs are also stronger."

The life spans for horses and donkeys are about equivalent—30 to 40 years. The cost of their care and feeding is also about the same.

What really set Sicilians apart, though, are their easygoing, loving temperaments.

"They're very affectionate animals," says Kathy MacGregor, Barbara's daughter and a fellow Sicilian owner. The Sicilians are visited by many schoolchildren who tour the

Pointe, Barbara's fourth-generation family ranch. "The kids go right into the stalls and play with them," says Kathy.

John K. Babb of Valley Exotics, an exotic-animal breeding farm in Paint Lick, Kentucky, has had similar experiences with his Sicilians. "They are so very affectionate and truly born that way. My donkeys always bray the second that I step out the door, sometimes to say they are hungry and other times just to say hello," he explains. "One of mine literally follows me around and flops his head on my hand, asking me to pet and scratch him. There exists, to my knowledge, no other equine equal in affectionate disposition to the miniature Sicilian donkey."

* * *

Winston on the Links

Today, miniature Sicilian donkeys are making increasing inroads in the United States and Canada as recreation and companion animals. They also make great "watchdogs." Because of their instinctive dislike of certain canine predators, Sicilians are now being employed as guards for herds of cattle or flocks of sheep. If a wolf, a coyote, or even a curious dog happens by, the donkeys will rear up and battle them off.

On her Canadian ranch, Barbara breeds and sells the Sicilian donkeys primarily as pets, though she points out, "They're still used by trekkers instead of llamas in mountainous regions. They're very strong and can carry big weights."

In Barbara's neck of the woods, though, the heaviest weights that Winston and his mates usually carry are small children and the occasional golf bag.

That's right. In addition to all of their other obligations and functions, miniature Sicilians can be assigned the task of dutifully and companionably caddying your clubs over the hills and greens of an 18-hole landscape. And if you don't feel like renting a golf cart, they'll also pull you along behind them in a small wagon. Is there anything that these amazing little creatures cannot do?

"Well, they're not so good at finding your golf balls," explains Barbara. "You'd have to unhitch them every time you lose one." ❂

chapter sixteen

The Caregiving Cure

If you walk into Judy Fay and Ralph McLaughlin's West Virginia home and stand very still and close your eyes, it almost seems as if you've been transported to the heart of a Brazilian rain forest. The high-pitched, silvery cries of exotic birds fill the air with such volume that Judy has to raise her voice to be heard.

The McLaughlins share their small home with 18 birds—almost all of them some variety of parrot. "At one time, we had as many as 32," Judy says, "But that was a little more than we could handle."

Judy is not just a fanatic for all things feathered; she also credits these birds, especially her first and favorite—Coa Coa—with helping her find the path to her own emotional healing after she faced the toughest news of her life.

But Coa Coa, a 4-year-old African Grey parrot with a snow-white face and a richly colored maroon tail, initially seemed like an unlikely savior.

After watching Judy lapse into a deep depression because of health problems, Ralph set out in search of a gift—any gift—that would bring back his wife's smile. "We had never owned a bird," Judy says, "but I had always wanted an African Grey. So, when Ralph found one at a flea market, we brought him home and named him Coa Coa."

The McLaughlins soon discovered, though, that the person who sold them Coa Coa had been less than honest about the bird's condition. "He almost died within the first 3 days that we had him," Judy recalls. "Yet, as much as he needed care and a home, he was terrified of people."

With a little detective work, Judy and Ralph tracked down several of Coa Coa's previous owners and discovered that in his own way, little Coa Coa had suffered almost as much as Judy was suffering. Because of misguided attempts at discipline and training, the bird had been repeatedly beaten, starved, and shuttled from owner to owner, until he eventually landed in a flea market.

Once the reasons for Coa Coa's fears and poor health became clear, Judy says, "I looked at him, and I realized that the little guy needed me as much as I needed him."

● ● ●

The Road to Wellness

Judy's severe bouts of depression began after she learned that her health problems could lead to only three possible outcomes: limited mobility with severe pain, confinement to a wheelchair, or being bedridden. To complicate matters further, doctors found that she had a rare blood disorder that made it difficult for her to take medication.

"All I had to look forward to was pain," she says. "I had reached the point where I was too depressed to leave the house." At best, the couple hoped that Coa Coa would be company for Judy. As first-time bird owners, they had no idea that a parrot could also be a source of tremendous love and compassion.

But soon enough, Judy found out what a tremendous inspiration Coa Coa could be. "It's hard to explain. But I somehow came to feel that my pain was nothing compared with what this little bird had been through," she says. Slowly, Coa Coa and Judy worked to win each other's confidence. "For the first 2 weeks, we kept his cage right next to where I sat. I'd talk to him all during the day, but for months, I did not dare to touch him," she recalls.

For Coa Coa's part, shy as he was, he found himself drawn to Judy's warmth and care. "I couldn't pick him up, but if his cage door was open and I left the room, he would follow me and call out, 'Momma, where you going?' I began to think, 'What am I doing feeling bad about myself when this bird has been through so much but is still trying?'" Judy says. "As he got better, I began to feel better, too."

Judy's concern for Coa Coa soon translated into an interest in the plight of other birds. "I talked to people and pet shop owners and found that, for many exotic birds, the abuse begins as soon as they are captured. Exporters often crowd as many as 20 birds into a small crate and ship them to the United States.

"In many cases, only 2 out of 10 make it here alive," Judy says. "Even after they become pets, it seems that people do not defend or understand birds the way they do dogs or cats. So they are often mistreated or given away."

As Coa Coa gained strength and Judy realized what a miraculous effect a loving environment could have on a wounded pet, she and Ralph decided to open their home to other birds in need. "Pet shop owners began to call me when no one else would take a bird because it was supposedly an unsuitable pet," she says.

These days, no matter what condition the birds are in on arrival, Judy does her best to nurture them back to good mental and physical health, even when they bite. "Sometimes I end up with stitches, but I stick with them until they're fit for a good home. I hold on to the worst cases," she says.

So, what is Judy's reward? "Some mornings, I wake up and I can hardly walk," she says, "But if can just get to where the birds are, they'll sing or they'll fly over and peck me on the cheek. Seeing a bird that was abused and afraid, but that will now snuggle up to me . . . that's love."

● ● ●

The Wisdom of Pets with Wings

To the uninitiated, Judy's special connection with birds may seem unusual. But avian-behavior expert Sally Blanchard, of Alameda, California, sees it a little differently. "Most people who have not had birds think that they are cold." In fact, says Blanchard, who is also the editor of *Pet Bird Report* magazine, "Many birds will recognize and respond to verbal cues and body language in ways that dogs and cats cannot. If you look into their eyes, you can see that being with a bird is as close to being with a person as you can get with a pet," she says.

Every pet owner thinks that his or her pet's breed is brilliant, but it seems that birds really do go to the head of the class when it comes to intelligence. "They're incredibly smart," says Irene M. Pepperberg, Ph.D., associate professor in both the psychology department and the ecology and evolutionary biology department at the University of Arizona in Tucson.

"Parrots, for example, live as long as 60 years. In that span of time, they learn to deal with complex social situations. They then bring this knowledge to their relationships with humans," says Dr. Pepperberg, whose most famous study subject is an African Grey who can distinguish objects by shape, color, or size and request them by name.

Parrots are also able to do more than mimic their owners' conversations. "They can make basic sentence frames and select words from their vocabulary to speak with you," says Dr. Pepperberg. On that subject, Judy would certainly agree. "When it's mealtime, Coa Coa takes it upon himself to call our dog over to his cage to pick up dropped pieces of food," Judy says.

From an emotional standpoint, it seems that Judy is also correct when she says that her birds give her love and affection. "Parrots are highly empathetic," says Blanchard. "If you feel bad, they feel bad. They are like emotional mirrors. If you have an abused bird who is suddenly given to someone who sees him as a sentient being, his behavior will change. It would not be a stretch," Blanchard continues, "to say that Judy's birds do love her. They feel bonded, and they are showing their appreciation."

Judy's analysis of her avian friends' impact on her life is far more straightforward. "I thank Coa Coa for giving me my life back, and for giving me a chance to do something with my life as well," she says. ✪

chapter seventeen

A Trick Just in Time

What do you envision when you think of a guardian angel? Do you see halos and beams of golden light? Do you imagine a rich voice and a face filled with heavenly beauty?

Many people probably do. But Jo Ann Altsman has a different view. To her, a guardian angel has a decidedly rounder shape. It doesn't sprout sunbeams, but it does sprout coarse hair. And its voice is more of a squeal than a divine baritone.

You see, Jo Ann's guardian angel is a potbellied pig by the name of Lulu.

• • •

An Exotic Hero

Potbellied pigs come from exotic beginnings. Originally from the tropics of South Asia, where many folks consider potbellies worthy of worship, they made their way to Canada in the mid-1980s. From there they crossed into the United States.

Despite her well-traveled roots, Lulu fits right in at the Altsmans' Pennsylvania home. "Lulu was originally a 40th-birthday present for my daughter—my husband Jack's idea. The problem was, my daughter collected *porcelain* pigs, not the real thing," Jo Ann says.

A 4-pound piglet at the time, little Lulu made a great initial impression, but within a few weeks, Jack and Jo Ann discovered that daughter Jackie was not quite ready for a real, live pig of her own. So Lulu moved in with them.

Lulu adjusted to her new neighborhood with ease, training herself to use the family cat's litter box (the cat, Trick, is *still* mad, says Jo Ann) and quickly developing a rapport with the local kids. Since potbellied pigs can be trained like dogs, it was no surprise that Lulu soon learned that doing a few cute tricks would guarantee her a treat. "She learned that playing dead was a great way to get Pop-Tarts," Jo Ann says.

As it turned out, Lulu's skills as an entertainer would bring her—and Jo Ann—far more than just frequent visits from local elementary school children. Her carefully honed routine may have started as a way to get goodies, but on one fateful day, it would save Jo Ann's life.

• • •

A Cry for Help

In August of 1997, the Altsmans packed Lulu and their Siberian husky, Bear, into the car and drove off to the family's mobile home on Lake Erie's Presque Isle. One morning, a couple of days later, Jack rose early to indulge in his favorite pastime—fishing—leaving Jo Ann home with the pets. The events that unfolded over the next few hours still amaze the Altsmans, their neighbors, and the elementary school kids who gather around to see the hero pig.

"I woke up, attempted to get out of bed, and passed out almost immediately," Jo Ann says. "When I came to, I was aware of incredible pain in my left arm and side, and I was having trouble breathing. I continued to pass out and come to, all the while trying to drag myself near a window or door to yell for help. I knew exactly what was happening to me . . . it was my second heart attack in 2 years."

There was no phone in the trailer, but Jo Ann knew that there were almost a thousand people in the mobile-home park, so she figured that the odds were good that shouting through an open window would get someone's attention.

"I couldn't stand, but I managed to reach a clock that was on a low table, and I threw it through one of our windows in order to break it," says Jo Ann. "Once the window shattered, I used all of my strength to call for help."

By that time, she could no longer crawl or move. Bear was also barking as loud as he could, but no one was coming. Then it was Lulu's turn.

"Lulu came over, stood next to me, and put her face right up close to mine and squealed," says Jo Ann. "She then turned around and went out to the yard through the doggy door. The door was too small for her belly, and she evidently scraped her sides on the way out."

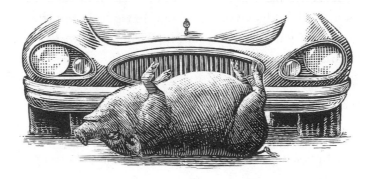

Jo Ann had no idea what Lulu was up to, but this was a pig with a plan. The 2-year-old, 150-pound porker ran out of the yard to the main road in front of the park. The Altsmans later discovered that, once Lulu was there, she lay down in the road—in the hopes of stopping a car. No one came.

Lulu returned to Jo Ann's side, then went back out to the road three times before she successfully corralled a concerned motorist. "The young man who finally stopped had to swerve when he saw what appeared to be a dead or injured animal in the road," Jo Ann says. It was Lulu, flat on her back with her hooves pointing skyward and her sides bloodied from three trips through the doggy door. She was doing her Pop-Tart trick—playing dead.

The driver stopped his car and ran over to Lulu. The pig immediately stood up and began to squeal and run toward the trailer. Concerned that he had hit the pig and wanting the owner to know that the animal was injured, he followed her.

"I heard him at my door saying, 'Hello . . . your pig's in distress.'" says Jo Ann. "He was close enough to hear me, so I said I needed an ambulance and that he needed to go to the park manager's office to get some help."

Doctors later told Jo Ann that she would not have lasted much longer. Lulu had summoned help just in time. Within days, Jo Ann had quintuple bypass surgery. Afterward, she was shocked to discover that Lulu, her gentle pet, had had to break the yard gate off its hinges in order to get out to the road.

● ● ●

A Princess among Pigs

Most people know very little about the behavior and intelligence of pigs, especially the potbellied variety. Perhaps that's why Lulu's noble behavior came as such a surprise to the Altsmans and their family and friends. Pigs, it seems, have been given a bad rap.

Two blockbuster *Babe* movies aside, we still think of them as pudgy little fellows who are interested only in wallowing in the mud. As it turns out, they're very smart pets and clean, too.

"Pigs in general are very intelligent," says Lisle George, D.V.M., Ph.D., a veterinarian and research scientist at the University of California, Davis, School of Veterinary Medicine who is an expert on all things porcine. "In fact, they tend to be more intellectual than dogs—they are thinkers."

Surprised? Dr. George says we shouldn't be. "We regularly underestimate the behavior of our pets—the animals that depend on us—since we provide their food and shelter. We think of them as children who are not very intelligent because we have never seen them on their own, in the wild. Often, we fail to see how willing they are to help us," he explains.

Superior intelligence and honorable intentions aside, Dr. George says Lulu is one exceptional pig. "My experience is that pigs are rather self-preserving. You wouldn't expect one to do a favor for you. This pig's behavior—putting herself out in the road—is somewhat unusual. Most pigs avoid stressful situations," he says.

But Margot Lasher, Ph.D., a psychologist in City Island, New York, and author of the book, *And the Animals Will Teach You*, thinks there may be an explanation.

Even if pigs are not just like dogs, Dr. Lasher says, "animals are especially attuned to emotions. Lulu may not have had any idea what a heart attack was, but she could feel the fear, the distress. She tapped into her owner's feelings and then decided to protect her."

Home from the hospital and back in good health, Jo Ann doesn't question Lulu's motives. "My husband believes, and I agree, that God sent us Lulu. She came to us for a reason," she says.

For her trouble, Lulu will probably never want for treats again. The ASPCA's national headquarters gave her an award for being a lifesaver. She has also become something of a local legend.

And elementary school kids love nothing better than to feed a legend Pop-Tarts. ⊙

chapter eighteen

Father, Mother, Friend, All in One

*M*ost male dogs won't stick around to play daddy after fathering a litter of pups. These carefree bachelors continue to prowl around the neighborhood, paying no mind to the females who feed and protect their offspring. They show no interest in nurturing the species' young, and they assume, it seems, that puppy rearing is simply not a male's work.

It's hardly evident that these deadbeat dads, considered the most civil of the canines, evolved from their wolf cousins. Every member of a wolf pack takes part in raising the pups. After a successful hunt, an adult male will return to the den to feed the young.

Not so with Peggy Callahan's German shepherd, Joshua. He clearly remembers the behaviors of his ancestors and has proven himself to be a capable parent. He doesn't even mind if it involves a different species. Nor does he mind when he is called upon to do a female's work.

Josh has spent 6 years serving as a surrogate parent to wolf pups at the Wildlife Science Center in Forest Lake, Minnesota. Peggy, the center's director, says that Josh steps in and helps raise baby wolves that the center breeds for zoos. His role, she explains, begins when the pups are removed from their mother. It continues until they are 6 months old and have jaws and claws with which he can't compete.

"He cares for them, licks them, and protects them," Peggy says.

It may sound like Josh is only playing at fatherhood or motherhood or whatever you want to call it, but Peggy says that his job is essential. The pups must be removed from their mothers 12 days after birth, before their eyes open, in order to get them comfortable with having people around. But still so young, the babies aren't ready to survive without a parent.

Newborn wolves can't urinate or defecate unless their genitals are stimulated. The adults lick the babies' genitals and actually consume the waste, Peggy says, so the cubs don't have to lie around in it. This is one of Josh's more unpleasant, but necessary, duties as a surrogate wolf-pup parent. But you won't catch him complaining.

Josh has other duties as well. When the wolf pups are bottle-fed by Wildlife Science Center staff members without an adult wolf nearby, they begin to get aggressive with each other, Peggy says. They're vying to establish a hierarchy of dominance within their little pack.

"I put Josh in with them to cap that aggression," she says. Dogs, like wolves, have certain gestures that show the pups who's the real boss. She has tried to imitate those gestures, "but people just can't pull it off."

When the pups get older and begin to recognize Joshua as their dear old dad, they show him when they are ready to eat solid food. "They will start to lick him on the nose, and he will start to regurgitate for them, to feed them. That's the most remarkable behavior that we see from Josh," Peggy says.

• • •

Born to Mother

"Josh was a yearling when I discovered his paternal nature," Peggy says. Or, is that maternal? His first show of parenthood wasn't with wolves, however.

Peggy was bottle-feeding bear cubs at the center, and several of her pet dogs were huddled around, interested in the tiny bears. Most of them backed off or started to growl at the cubs, she says. But not Josh.

"When I presented them to Josh, he started to lick his lips and whine, with no aggression." Then, the shepherd began to lick the cubs' faces, and he licked their genitals to stimulate urination.

There was no doubt that the young dog wanted to foster the bear cubs, Peggy says, so she put him to work with the wolves, a task more fitting to his genus and genius.

Joshua's nurturing nature doesn't appear only when he's around furry mammals, Peggy says. He has also bonded with her own baby, 5-month-old Megan, and treats her just like a pup.

Peggy and her husband, Mark Beckel, have 16 shepherds and 2 mutts. All but Josh and his brother Seamus were rescued from abusive homes or were found wandering the streets. Peggy and Mark bought Josh and Seamus as their wedding gifts to one another. While Seamus has also been helpful in keeping the wildlife center's baby wolves under control, his skills aren't quite as advanced as his brother's.

The Wildlife Science Center is home to gray wolves, red wolves, black bears, birds of prey, and other wild species native to Minnesota. It began as a federally funded wolf research center, Peggy says, but the federal funds eventually dried up, and the government announced that it was going to shut the center down.

As the center's director, Peggy was expected to kill its wildlife collection.

• • •

From Public to Private

Peggy and her employees were devastated by the thought of destroying all of the animals, along with everything they had worked for. So they decided to take over the facility and turn it into a nonprofit education center, targeting programs to schoolchildren. "I don't think anybody expected us to survive," she says, admitting that she herself often wondered how they would make ends meet.

Peggy soon took on a position at an area zoo to make money for vaccinations and food for the animals. Today, although it took several years of struggling, the center is a successful organization that seeks to educate the public about wolves.

Occasionally, Peggy will agree to breed a litter of pups if a reputable zoo requests it. "More people visit zoos in this country than attend sporting events," she says. That, she feels, is a great way to spread the word that the beautiful creatures deserve a better shot at survival.

Elizabeth Frank, curator of mammals for the Milwaukee County Zoo, took in a litter of the Wildlife Science Center's pups for a new Wolf Woods exhibit. Josh tagged along to help the small pack of five pups acclimate to their new home.

Peggy says that Josh's presence was important to the wolves as they made the transition to a new home. "Had we not taken Joshua, these pups would still be huddled for days afterward," she says. The pups were terrified of all of the people visiting the zoo, but seeing Josh close by eased their fears and allowed them to explore their new environment.

The wolves adapted to their new home quite well, Frank says, and they've become a popular addition to the zoo.

Frank, who has worked in zoos for 25 years, says that it is common for domestic animals to be companions for wild species. Once, in the National Zoo in Washington, D.C., Frank saw a rhinoceros befriend a pygmy goat.

But, she adds, friendship is one thing. It's something else entirely for a male dog to take on female duties for a whole different species.

But there aren't a lot of male dogs like Josh. ✪

chapter nineteen

The Bells of Saint Roc

Linda Matthews sat bolt upright in bed. "That one sounded awfully close," she told her husband, Rosevelt.

The bedside clock read 3:45 A.M. That meant that the thunderstorm had been raging for nearly 2 hours. The New Bern, North Carolina, couple had been able to sleep through most of it, but that last lightning bolt had lit up their bedroom as bright as day.

Rosevelt got up and unplugged the television set. Then he and Linda settled into their bed and tried to fall back to sleep.

Meanwhile, out in the backyard, Roc—their year-old Chesapeake Bay retriever–Rottweiler mix—lay watching the storm through his doghouse door. He, too, flinched at the noisy, too-close lightning strike.

But unlike Linda and Rosevelt, Roc wasn't interested in sleeping. Instead, he clambered out of his cozy, dry house and sniffed the wet air, sensing danger. His ears perked up. He loped across the large backyard to learn more.

"Is that Roc barking?" a drowsy Linda murmured to her husband.

"It sounds too far away," came Rosevelt's sleepy reply. "It must be a neighbor's dog."

But the barking wasn't a neighbor's dog. It was Roc. Something was terribly, terribly wrong, and he was trying his level best to let somebody know.

After about 20 minutes, Linda gave Rosevelt a nudge. "I'm sure that's Roc," she insisted. Besides being a loving and faithful companion, Roc was also an excellent watchdog. "Maybe there's someone hanging around outside," she suggested.

"I'll go take a look," Rosevelt replied and climbed out of bed to investigate.

While Rosevelt checked the front door and windows, Linda looked in on their two sons, Romaro and Sheldon. Both boys were sleeping soundly, despite the storm that still raged on.

● ● ●

How Roc Found a Family

Watching her boys sleep while Roc barked outside, Linda couldn't help recalling all the times that her younger son had asked whether he could have a dog. "I'd take good care of it," Sheldon had always promised, but Linda had suspected differently.

"Sooner or later, I'll be the one who winds up responsible for feeding and walking any dog we might get," she had always insisted.

And then, one day, Sheldon tagged along when his mom headed out for her daily 2-mile walk. "You know, Mom, every boy my age wants a dog of his own," he said when they were a few blocks from home.

He was quiet for a long moment. Then, in a choked voice, he added, "Every Christmas morning, the very first thing I always do is look to see if maybe this year there's a puppy under the tree for me."

Linda's heart melted. And so, the day that Sheldon came home overjoyed because his friend's dog had just had pups, she finally said yes.

Linda's reverie was interrupted by yet another flash of lightning and crash of thunder. "There's no one outside but Roc," Rosevelt said, appearing in the hallway at his wife's side. "I imagine he's just upset about all the noise. Come on, let's go back to sleep."

"Do you think he's cold, running around in the rain like that?" Linda asked as she snuggled between the bedsheets.

"He's fine," Rosevelt assured her. All the same, Linda figured, as soon as the rain let up, she'd slip outside and towel Roc dry.

But Roc wasn't fine. He was terrified by the thunderstorm, even though the tempest was secondary in his mind at that point. Roc was a dog on a mission, and he was growing increasingly desperate to make someone understand what was happening. And if barking wasn't working, well, he'd just have to try something else.

● ● ●

Roc Gets Creative

Roc bounded onto the patio and pawed at the sliding glass door. He tried standing on his hind legs so that he could scratch with both paws, but the glass was slippery, and he kept falling over. And so he moved to one side and attacked the wooden trim beside the door. He yelped and scratched, and then he did something he'd done once before when he wanted Sheldon to come out and play.

"Who on earth could be ringing the doorbell at this hour?" Linda wondered as she threw off the sheets and climbed out of bed. That was when she saw it—a faint orange reflection in the bedroom window. "I never would have seen it if I hadn't gotten up to see who was ringing that doorbell," Linda remembers.

Rosevelt spotted the orange glow, too. "The house is on fire!" he shouted.

The couple rushed to their boys' bedroom and woke them up. Then the family hurried out the front door and across the street to a neighbor's. Glancing back, Linda was

horrified to see her entire roof collapsing into the one-story house.

The Matthewses' house had been struck by lightning. Because the fire had started on the roof and because heat rises, their smoke alarms had been unable to detect the rapidly spreading flames.

Linda had already guessed that it was Roc who had rung the back doorbell. "If he hadn't, we still would have been lying in bed when the ceiling came down on top of us in flames," she recalls with a visible shudder. "None of us would have made it out alive."

While Linda used the neighbor's phone to call 911, Roosevelt went back for Roc. He opened the gate and hurried around the house. Roc was still there on the patio. But he was no longer barking or scratching at the door.

The fire was now visible through the glass, as one room after another ignited into flames. Roc watched it happening, whimpering and trembling and doubtless thinking that he'd failed his family.

"Here, boy!" Roosevelt called, and when Roc spotted him, the 75-pound pooch dashed over, virtually leaping into Roosevelt's arms.

The fire department arrived within minutes, but it was already too late. By then, the Matthewses' house was one giant fireball. Moments later, it collapsed inward, showering flaming debris everywhere. It was everything firefighters could do just to keep the flames from spreading to other homes nearby.

Across the street, Roc was no longer watching the flames. He barked and jumped and licked everyone's face. "You saved our lives, boy," Sheldon told him, burying his face in his best friend's sodden fur.

Loyalty Overcomes Fear

"Thunderstorms can be very frightening events for dogs, especially if they're outside and alone," observes Tom Fore, D.V.M., a veterinarian in Richmond, Virginia. "Roc could have stayed safely huddled inside his doghouse, but, like so many of our canine friends, he chose to put himself at the very bottom of the totem pole that night.

"It didn't matter that he was probably trembling with fear. When Roc sensed danger, he put his own welfare aside and did everything he could to alert his family."

How many people would do the same? According to Dr. Fore, "This is just one of the reasons why dogs truly are man's best friend."

And woman's, too. "We lost everything, but we were all safe, thanks to Roc," says Linda. "He's our family hero, and none of us will ever forget what he did that night." ✪

chapter twenty

Rocky Meets His Bullwinkle

When Bill Goss was 9 years old, he nearly drowned in a sink. Afterward, he picked himself up, brushed himself off, and breathed a huge sigh of relief. It would be far from the last time that he felt that way.

Over the next 30 years, Bill came face-to-face with death in as many times. He found himself dangling from the side of a mountain, a fingertip away from oblivion. He walked away from a mine cave-in. An encounter with high explosives nearly did him in. Another time, he found himself at the wrong end of a gun and a near miss away from doom.

When he was hit by a speeding car, for instance, his body sailed 45 feet while his soul watched it all in amazement from above. He hit the ground, woke up, and realized with relief that he was still alive. It was all over in about 5 seconds, and he couldn't have been afraid for more than 2 of those seconds because, frankly, he barely knew what had hit him.

It's little wonder that Bill had always firmly believed that the touch of a kindred spirit held tremendous healing power. He also believed that good friends, strong faith, family support, a clear mind, and a sense of humor were all a guy needed to survive.

But little did Bill know that, when faced with his most dreadful brush with death, he would find the necessary moral support to overcome it from a friend who fit in his pocket.

• • •

The Toughest Challenge Yet

As with being struck by a car, most of Bill's calamities were over in minutes, if not seconds. Then came a life-threatening situation that lasted 5 long years.

It began when he was 38 years old and an award-winning Navy pilot. He had just broken the sound barrier in an F-18 Hornet. "I've had that dream since I was a small boy," Bill says of his supersonic achievement.

But his celebration was cut tragically short. The next day he was introduced to a foe that was determined to test every ounce of his strength: amelanotic melanoma, one of the deadliest forms of skin cancer.

"I found a tiny little bump on the back of my left ear," Bill says, describing the growth as being pea-size and hard, but the color of normal skin.

He went to a military flight surgeon to have the growth removed, but she told him not to bother; it looked like it was just a harmless cyst. He left her office, considered the matter, and then returned the same day, demanding that she cut it off.

"For some reason, I don't know why, I wanted this thing off my ear," he says. "I said, 'Listen, if you don't cut this off my ear, I'm going to cut it off in the bathroom with a straight razor.'"

That caught the surgeon's attention, and she quickly re-moved the cyst.

A week later, a doctor who had examined the cyst told Bill that he had a rare form of cancer and was likely to die within 6 months.

But since he had not let 30 other catastrophes kill him, Bill wasn't about to let a few out-of-control cancer cells get the best of him. He underwent surgery immediately.

During a 12-hour operation, Bill's face, neck, ear, and throat were peeled off and cut apart until his cancer cells and lymph nodes, half his ear, and some muscles were gone. "They tore the left side of my face off," he says. "It wasn't a pretty picture. I ended up looking like Frankenstein."

● ● ●

Rocky Flies to the Rescue

To say that Bill was down in the dumps is a gross understate-ment. He didn't feel very pretty, either. The operation left painful scars that required him to spend a great deal of time moping on morphine.

And then Rocky dropped in.

Rocky was unlike any practitioner of the healing arts that Bill had ever known. He had no stethoscope, no degree, and, in fact, no clothes. Who needs them when you're a flying squirrel?

A good friend, John Rossi, D.V.M., presented Rocky to Bill, claiming that the orphaned baby squirrel had fallen out of a tree and needed his help to survive the trauma.

"In actuality," Bill says, "he also knew that having to take care of a baby squirrel would be a wonderful distraction for me."

Rocky appeared at Dr. Rossi's Jacksonville, Florida, veteri-nary clinic after he was found lying orphaned by the roadside.

"We treat a lot of injured wildlife," Dr. Rossi says, naming tortoises and flying squirrels as some of the more common wild species that he spends his time mending.

Dr. Rossi even had a pet flying squirrel of his own that Bill had met before his bout with cancer. "Bill got a real kick out of it," he recalls.

Rocky, then no bigger than a walnut, somehow seemed to know right away where he was needed most. He checked out the deep scars running down Bill's face and neck and did what came naturally to him. He curled up and went to sleep on them.

It was this touch, Bill says, that inspired him to buck up and kick the cancer. "There I was, feeling this tiny little warm cotton ball, this tiny little heart beating right on top of where my jugular vein used to be," he says. From there, he didn't look back.

"Rocky helped me have the right attitude," Bill says. "I was a flyer also, so we related just on the flying alone."

• • •

A Miraculous Mate for Mending

Flying squirrels, about the size of gerbils but gray with bulging eyes and glider wings, tend to make amicable pets, says Dr. Rossi. Plus, they're generally very gentle animals. They will eat out of a person's hand and travel in his pocket. They will even climb an owner's body like a tree trunk.

"It's sort of like a hamster on steroids," Dr. Rossi says.

When the homeless and orphaned Rocky was brought into his clinic, Dr. Rossi's wife, Roxanne, suggested that the little rodent would be a good gift for Bill, who had just returned home from his surgery. "We knew that Bill was going through some difficult times," he says. But they never expected quite the response they got.

Dr. Rossi says that Bill's spirits were so lifted by the baby squirrel that his bond with Rocky played a large role in saving his life. He has seen other evidence of significant human-animal bonds, but he believes that Rocky and Bill have one of the strongest.

Bill is the first to agree. As soon as he took Rocky into his home and his life, the nocturnal animal took to having early-morning coffee klatches with Bill just before his own bedtime. Rocky liked to perch on the scars on top of Bill's head, eating pecans while his owner read the newspaper.

When Bill finished his coffee and Rocky finished his nuts, the squirrel would climb down Bill's head, following the deep scars from his left ear around his head, down his neck, and across his left shoulder. He would then fall asleep comfortably burrowed under Bill's bathrobe, alongside a scar. Bill says that he never trained the tiny rodent to walk along his wounds; Rocky just preferred to dwell on those painful places.

Now, in his current occupation as a motivational speaker, Bill tells crowds about his five "Fs" of fulfillment: family, friends, faith, focus, and fun. "If we utilize these things, we can overcome any adversity," he says. "And Rocky was right in there. He helped me with all those things."

Bill, his wife Peggy, their twins Brian and Christie, and a houseful of other pets still enjoy Rocky's company in Orange Park, Florida.

Rocky lives in a tall birdcage in the kitchen and wakes up for dinner at six o'clock in the evening. He begs for table scraps, Bill says, though he doesn't eat much. The squirrel fills up on one tiny bean, one grape, or a pecan. Then he's up all night long, chirping until the family rises for breakfast.

Five-and-a-half years after his surgery, Bill doesn't have a trace of cancer, and an observer would never guess from a glance at his face that it was once torn apart. "Doctors say that they have never seen scars heal so quickly," Bill says.

He now spends his time teaching others around the world how to get through their own crises. He maintains a Web site, has appeared on television talk shows and radio shows with his buddy Rocky, and has a book detailing his ordeals and subsequent triumphs.

That same book, *The Luckiest Unlucky Man Alive*, was reenacted on a television show in Japan. It's even being considered as a future Hollywood movie.

Throughout all the requests for interviews, Rocky tends to be the harder one to contact. That's because interviews are usually done during the day, his normal bedtime. And he's curled up, asleep, on Bill. ✪

chapter twenty-one

Love Truly Is Blind

On the surface, it seems like any other modern storybook romance: Lucy met her match through the Internet. She traveled thousands of miles to join the handsome gentleman. The two were acquainted and a brief courtship ensued. Now she plans to stay by his side forever.

Yes, for this little lady, it was clearly love at first sight.

But from the perspective of her beau, Barry, that's not exactly how events unfolded.

Oh, yes, he fell in love instantly—just not in the way you might imagine. Barry wasn't able to see Lucy's perky little nose or her gorgeous black-and-white fur coat. He couldn't make eyes at her as he introduced himself.

No, Barry's attraction was more like love at first scent, sound, and whisker-touch. Barry is blind. And although he couldn't see Lucy, he knew right away that she was the one for him.

Some Bunny to Love

Neither Barry nor Lucy is a creature of the human variety. Barry is a 7-pound, one-eyed Lop rabbit mix who was adopted from the San Diego chapter of the House Rabbit Society, a national education, adoption, and fostering organization. Lucy is a svelte, 5-pound Dutch rabbit who hails from Michigan. Besides her penchant for giving kisses, she displays her caring side in a most remarkable way.

You might say Lucy is a Seeing Eye bunny and, quite literally, the light of Barry's life. Though she can't read him the morning paper or get him safely across a busy intersection, Lucy does things for Barry that he appreciates even more.

She grooms him and bathes him, meticulously cleaning the part of his face where his left eye used to be. She guides him and nudges him in the directions he needs to go, helping him take care of the important business of life—namely eating, sleeping, cuddling, and eating some more.

And if ever Barry should stumble as he scrambles toward the delightful sound of treats destined for his little belly, Lucy runs back to help him, momentarily forgoing her own treat to stop and assist her furry soul mate.

"She's his eyes," says the rabbits' caretaker, Kristin Felsburg, who lives with Lucy and Barry (and her husband, Mike) in Royal Oak, Michigan. "It's amazing to watch them. Lucy knows that there is something different about Barry, and she just takes care of him."

And even though Lucy and Kristin have always shared a close relationship—complete with kiss-filled greetings and quiet times on the couch together—Kristin knows better than to come between her bunny buddies. Lucy is extremely serious about her role as Barry's caretaker, as Kristin discovered one day when she knelt down to help Barry.

"Lucy came running over and started butting my hand with her head, kind of like, 'No, no, no, you get away. I'll take care of him. That's my job.'"

• • •

Learning to Care

Perhaps Lucy picked up her maternal ways from the people in her life, who pamper her with the same care and affection that many people reserve for cats and dogs. Even Kristin's decision to adopt a second rabbit in 1997 was based on her concern for Lucy.

With a full-time job quickly approaching, Kristin worried that Lucy might become too lonely if left by herself all day. As Kristin prepared to graduate from college and relocate for a while from Michigan to California, she also launched a search for a new addition to the family.

As it turned out, she didn't have to look for long. Around the country, rabbits are often acquired as impulse purchases

and later surrendered to animal shelters and rabbit fostering groups. A quick Internet search turns up not only the House Rabbit Society and its many chapters but also descriptions of bunny after bunny in need of a home.

A bit like personal ads, these descriptions sometimes include pictures, sometimes not. But they always detail a few vital statistics. The description of Barry on the Web site was only a brief profile, but it didn't need to be any longer to capture Kristin's heart.

Already named Barry, as in "barry cute," the little fellow hadn't had an easy time of it in his 3 short years. Barry had been abandoned by his owners, who had dropped him off at an animal hospital for eye treatment and never returned to pick him up.

He'd been treated repeatedly for abscesses in both eyes, caused by systemic infections stemming from bacteria in his bloodstream. Eventually, he went blind. Later, he lost his left eye altogether when it had to be surgically removed because of infection.

Although many people would be overwhelmed by the idea of caring for such a needy animal, Kristin couldn't bear the thought of *not* caring for him.

"I've always had a soft spot for those who don't quite have it all or who are a little bit disadvantaged. When I saw Barry's story, I just knew that nobody was ever going to want to take him in," she says. "I knew there was the possibility of future medical problems and medical bills, but my heart just went out to him, and I thought, 'Well, he needs a home, and Lucy needs a good friend.'"

● ● ●

Matchmaker, Make Me a Match

Before she could welcome Barry into her home, however, Kristin had to get Lucy's seal of approval. Rabbits are social animals who often enjoy each other's company, but they can also be extremely protective of their territory. To ensure domestic bliss in a multiple-rabbit household, rabbit aficionados sometimes go to great lengths to help the bunnies bond.

Barry and Lucy were fortunate enough to have an experienced matchmaker on their side in the form of Libby Donovan. Libby was not only Barry's foster mom but also the founding manager of the House Rabbit Society's San Diego chapter.

After rescuing and caring for scores of homeless rabbits, Libby was well-prepared for the intricacies of bunny behavior. The first step in bonding, she says, is to place two bunny strangers together in unfamiliar territory, where they are both fish out of water.

"Rabbits, like people, are individuals," she says. "Sometimes it's love at first sight, and sometimes it takes a couple of days to a week to get them accustomed to one another. Sometimes it takes a year or more, if they have really strong personalities."

For Barry and Lucy, the bonding process took only as long as a hop, a skip, and a jump—and a 20-mile car ride from the hotel where Kristin spent her first night in California. Sitting in a cardboard box in the backseat of Libby's car, Barry and Lucy clung to each other for support. By the time they were back on stable ground in Libby's home, they already appeared inseparable.

Within 3 days, the bunnies were ready for their new life together. "Lucy just completely accepted Barry," says Libby. "She took one look at him and went, 'Oh, hi!' He was very much a gentleman. He really welcomed having another bunny there to help him identify where things were. He could relate to her. They were instant companions."

They've rarely left each other's side since. Wherever Lucy goes, Barry is not far behind, practically stepping on the heels of his companion—and sometimes outrunning her if the smell of rabbit treats is in the air. The two love bunnies even make a date of going to the veterinarian: When Lucy was spayed, the already-neutered Barry spent the night with her as she recovered at the animal hospital.

● ● ●

Fun Needs No Vision

Even though Barry depends on Lucy to help him get around, he's certainly no shrinking violet. In fact, if the little guy could talk, he might be inclined to brag that he's been wildly successful at hopping over the hurdles of his disability. And amazingly enough, Barry is the dominant bunny.

Whereas Lucy likes to share her treats, Barry's manners are a bit less refined. "If I have an apple core, Barry yanks it away from me and goes running around in circles," says Kristin. "She shares, but he doesn't. Barry doesn't just sit there and be blind. He definitely has his fun."

And eyes aside, Barry's senses are as sharp as he needs them to be. His ears are well-tuned to the sound of a refrigerator door opening—a noise that has often sent him scurrying into the kitchen with Lucy.

Barry responds to his own name just as a dog would. And his whiskers and nostrils work in tandem, helping him dodge misplaced objects. When he has to adjust to a new arrangement, he just keeps making slow, careful circles, starting small and expanding the spiral until he has mapped out the whole room. Then it's smooth sailing—or leaping—from there.

"He won't smack into anything unless he hears treats. Then he just takes off," says Kristin. "Every now and then, when he's really excited, he'll bump into something . . . but it doesn't faze him too much."

• • •

Making Use of Multiple Senses

Despite their reputation for keen eyesight, rabbits can't see very well up close and, in fact, make significant use of other senses, says Jeffrey Jenkins, D.V.M., the San Diego veterinarian who performed the eye surgery on Barry. A specialist in birds and exotic animals who has been around rabbits since he got his first pet bunny as a child, he says that rabbits focus best on things that are coming at them from far away.

"They use their senses of smell and hearing a lot more than people do, and rabbits can smell in a way that I don't even know that we comprehend well," Dr. Jenkins says. "They smell three-dimensionally. They can smell that you're over there and I'm over here and that the dog walked across the room in that direction. Literally, there's probably a time component to their ability to smell. And so those things all help Barry. As long as somebody doesn't rearrange the furniture, he does pretty well."

So well, in fact, that he has stolen Lucy's heart—and her attentions—away from Kristin. "Lucy used to be really attached to me, and now she just totally ignores me because she's so attached to Barry," Kristin says, laughing. "She used to follow me around and jump on my bed and sleep with me at night."

Now lady Lucy gives the lion's share of her time to Barry. When the Felsburgs come home from work and bring Lucy downstairs to play, she'll humor them for a little while, but she soon hops back upstairs to check on Barry, who prefers to stay where he's most familiar with the lay of the land.

But it's not all cold shoulders for Kristin. In fact, Lucy still likes to find her way to Kristin's shoulder from time to time, hopping up onto the back ledge of the couch and working her way toward Kristin's face in the hopes of getting a lick of ice cream. And every night when Kristin comes home from work, Lucy runs to the baby gate that keeps the bunnies safely confined in their bedroom to give her human friend a passionate, slobbery greeting. "I'll lie down on the ground with her, and she'll just give me a bath," says Kristin.

It's a pampered life for these two love bunnies—and why not? After all, they were the champions of the Michigan Humane Society's 1999 "My Pet Is a Hero" contest.

"I promote two rabbits as heroes today," Kristin wrote in her winning essay. "First, Barry for the courageous struggle that he undergoes daily against a dark world. And second, his female friend, Lucy, for her dedication to Barry and for her nurturing instinct to guide him through what he doesn't know. They live with something that most other animals—and even most people—can't understand."

And who wouldn't deserve a treat for that? ✪

chapter twenty-two

Bravery on the River

If there's one thing that history has proved, it's that the underdog should never be counted out. There's the case of David and Goliath. The tortoise and the hare. Holly and the deer.

Holly and the deer? Yes, this is a modern-day fable of the weak against the strong, the little against the big. And this one involves a real underdog.

One sunny Saturday afternoon in June, Norma Myers and her granddaughter, Alicia, were taking Holly, a 13-year-old springer spaniel, for a stroll by the banks of the Similkameen River near their home in Princeton, British Columbia, Canada.

Norma says that Ally, as she affectionately calls her 4-year-old granddaughter, loves to spend time with Holly. "She says that Holly is her dog, and that I just look after Holly when she's not around."

As it turned out on this day, it was Holly who was looking after Ally.

Fury from the Forest

Ally was playing a few steps ahead of Norma and Holly, dancing along the river's edge and showing them how fast she could run through the grass. The spring day suddenly turned terrifying. Without warning, a wild-eyed female deer leapt out of the woods.

Then, the doe stormed toward Ally.

"It just came right through the fence. There was nothing we could do," Norma says. "I was shocked. When I screamed, Holly looked up to see what was the matter. And she ran right for the deer. She got between the deer and Ally. She was barking and jumping at the deer."

Ally didn't even see the deer before Holly stepped in to stop it, Norma says. Holly worked furiously to keep the doe from Alicia. Her tactics worked. The doe halted, its attention turned toward the dog.

It was Holly who then took the brunt of the deer's anger. Although the little dog was successful in keeping the doe from harming the child, it managed to stomp all over Holly.

That didn't stop the dog from continuing to bark and nip at the deer's heels, Norma says. Holly wouldn't give up, injured though she was. Norma began swatting at the deer with Holly's leash. Together, she and the spaniel worked to beat it back. But the doe still wasn't intimidated enough to run away.

Norma then realized that she was holding a full can of root beer. So she shook it up, popped the top, and sprayed soda all over the doe, finally her scaring her back into the woods.

But the ordeal wasn't over. Holly was lying on the ground with a broken leg, a swollen eye, and contusions all over her small body. The nearest veterinary hospital was 1½ hours away. Norma didn't think the dog would make it. "She wasn't making any noises. I was so scared."

Ally was scared, too. "She was crying, because she loved Holly," says Norma.

They rushed the dog to an animal hospital in Penticton, where Steve Harvey, D.V.M., mended her broken leg and treated her other wounds.

Dr. Harvey says that Holly certainly took the brunt of the deer's attack. The dog wasn't in good shape when she showed up in his office, but she showed an amazing will to pull through. She healed remarkably quickly, he says.

As impressed as he was by her physical strength, Dr. Harvey was equally struck by her courage in protecting Ally. "It was a wonderful story, a lifesaving event," he says.

• • •

A Covenant from the Past

Dogs and humans have had close links for thousands of years, Dr. Harvey says, and the dog's strong bond with its human family brings out the animal's natural instinct of protecting its own. "Our dogs don't roam around in packs anymore," he says. "They run around with families. People who have dogs understand. Your family becomes their pack."

Many people in Princeton were surprised at the doe's aggressive behavior, Dr. Harvey says, because deer attacks are rare indeed. But female deer do sometimes display aggression in the spring, when they have young. The mother must have been protecting her young, he surmises.

And Holly, well, she was doing the same.

Though she was an older dog, Holly had been living with Norma for only 2½ years when she showed her devotion by saving Ally's life. Norma had inherited Holly from an elderly woman who had moved into a senior citizen apartment that allowed no pets.

"I thought twice about taking an older dog," Norma says, explaining that she had originally feared that the spaniel wouldn't get along with her grandchildren. But Holly proved herself to be a loving pal to the old and the young alike.

Though she adores small children—especially Ally, Norma says—Holly has also spent lots of time brightening the lives of elderly folks at the nursing home where Norma used to work as the director. Holly's not the kind of dog who likes to stay alone for too long, so she went to the nursing home with Norma each day to keep the residents company.

"She was thoroughly spoiled," Norma says. The residents doted on her with treats and lots of petting.

But Norma admits that she can't blame the nursing home residents for treating Holly too well, because she gets most of her pampering right at home. "We look at Holly as a little person with fur," Norma says.

Her leg won't completely heal, and she has taken on a slight limp. She tires out earlier than she used to. But Norma knows that Holly is not afraid to go back down by the river and resume her daily walks.

"She'll go anywhere I go," Norma says. And she'll always be ready to jump in and protect those whom she loves. ❂

chapter twenty-three

The Case of the
Thunderstruck Terrier

It was a dark and stormy afternoon in Decatur, Georgia. Like Snoopy banished to his doghouse, P. D., a 5½-year-old, 30-pound Jack Russell terrier mix, was home alone. She was not a happy pup.

Ever since she was struck by a hit-and-run driver and lost a leg and part of her jaw, P. D. has been terrified of loud noises—especially thunderstorms. "If I'm home with her, she's fine," says Abbi Taylor Guest, P. D.'s owner. "But if she's by herself, she becomes frantic and tears up the house trying to get out."

During this particular downpour, P. D. somehow managed to gnaw her way through the bolt lock on a set of French doors. Confused, disoriented, and terrified, she bounded across the yard and into the road. And straight into the path of a DeKalb County animal-control officer.

Later that afternoon, when Abbi called home to check her answering machine, there was a message from the animal-

126

control department alerting her to the fact that P. D. had been taken into custody. Abbi hurried to the pound and paid $23 to bail her buddy out of the clink. But then, Abbi was presented with a pair of $75 citations—one for failing to keep her pet under restraint and a second for allowing her to run at large.

Abbi tried explaining to the animal-control officer about how P. D. had chewed her way out of the house and about how terrified she was of thunderstorms. The officer's response? "Tell it to the judge."

Abbi decided to do just that. But first, she had an idea.

● ● ●

In the Name of the Law

Abbi, who at the time was a county public defender, had spent the afternoon of her canine's incarceration accompanying a client to the Georgia Mental Health Institute to have him evaluated for a possible defense of not guilty by reason of insanity. A few days later, when she visited the institute again to pick up some paperwork, she made a special point of seeking out Robert Storms, Ph.D.

Dr. Storms is the institute's forensics director, the man in charge of providing mental-health evaluations for DeKalb County residents who have been charged with crimes. Abbi told the psychologist all about P. D.'s legal plight and described her traumatic past. Dr. Storms was sympathetic. Half joking, he remarked, "You understand, don't you, that I couldn't possibly conduct an official evaluation without a face-to-face interview?"

Abbi smiled. "P. D. just happens to be right outside in my car."

A few weeks later, Abbi appeared at the recorder's court of the Stone Mountain judicial circuit, with the Honorable Robert Sneed presiding. When P. D.'s case was called, Abbi stood up and asked to address the court.

"First of all, I'd like to express my sincere appreciation to the animal-control officer for picking up my puppy and keeping her safe." Then, she turned to face the judge. "I respectfully request permission to offer a plea of not guilty due to temporary insanity," she said, offering her supporting paperwork to the court clerk.

Exhibit A consisted of a psychiatric-evaluation report from Dr. Storms. In it, he wrote, "P. D. has a history of intense anxiety behavior related to thunderstorms. On the day of the arrest, there was severe thunder and lightning and a rainstorm.

"A resultant, intense anxiety led her to flee and run around blindly in terror. It is our opinion that she was so overwhelmed by fear that she was unable to distinguish between right and wrong. While she may not have been acting under a delusional compulsion, her reality-orientation was significantly impaired. She should not be held accountable for her actions."

Transcripts reveal that Judge Sneed had but a single question for Anthony Carter, the animal-control officer who had nabbed P. D. "Was the dog good-natured when you picked her up?"

Under oath, Carter testified that when he opened his door, P. D. had leapt into the truck's front seat, where she had calmly remained during the entire trip to the pound. It was the very first time that the officer had ever allowed an animal to ride shotgun.

Banging down his gavel, the judge threw out the fines and reduced the charges to warnings.

● ● ●

A Friend of the Court

"I was impressed both with Ms. Guest's presentation and with her creativity," relates Judge Sneed, who frequently adjudicates pet-related cases in his courtroom. "But more important, I had to consider the circumstances surrounding the incident, and the dog herself."

According to Judge Sneed, P. D. had not truly misbehaved. Nor had she caused any injury by her actions. "The animal had developed a phobia, and she was simply looking for help," he observes. "Sometimes, in the pursuit of justice, you have to follow the spirit and not the letter of the law."

In a posttrial statement, Abbi promised to bolt her doors more securely from then on. "Thanks to the court's compassionate judgment, I'm sure P. D. will be able to overcome her many challenges," she said.

To help her meet those challenges, Abbi also bought P. D. a playmate—a 45-pound pug named Spanky. The two became quick friends. Nowadays, on dark and stormy afternoons, instead of chewing up the door frames, P. D. curls up in her dog bed and sleeps tightly alongside her new furry friend. ✪

chapter twenty-four

A Bratty Cat Saves a Life

*W*atching television, 15-year-old Jose Ybarra doesn't notice Brat the cat padding stealthily across the back of the sofa.

Closer. Closer. Then, suddenly, a jet-black paw reaches out and cuffs him on the ear. "Hey!" Jose exclaims. He makes a grab, but already the cat is halfway across the room—sitting on the carpet in front of the television and batting her luminous green eyes as if to say, "How dare you pay attention to anything else but me!"

Jose scoops the cat into his arms and feels her throaty purr against his chest. "We sure picked the right name for you, didn't we, Brat?" he says with a smile.

From the moment he first laid eyes on the tiny stray, Jose sensed that there was something special about this kitten. But in his wildest dreams, he never imagined that one day soon, he would owe his very life to his furry new friend.

For his 15th birthday, Jose had asked for only one gift—a playful kitten to call his own. He and his mom, Karen Hummerich, visited numerous breeders and pet stores, but none of the kittens ever seemed quite right to Jose.

"The kitten I want will be the one that I just can't imagine not taking home with us," he told his mom.

Then, one afternoon, Jose and his mom visited a local pet shop and spotted a black tabby with a white blaze on its chest. "Someone found her in an abandoned car and brought her to us," the store owner said, handing the scruffy orphan to Jose.

As soon as the kitten curled up in Jose's arms, purring, he knew. "This is my cat."

The kitten made herself right at home in the family's Wheeling, Illinois, apartment. She explored every nook and cranny. She dashed down the hallway, leaping into the air and ricocheting off walls in a frenzy of delight. She pounced on family members' feet at every opportunity. "You are such a brat," Karen laughed once, after the kitten batted her playfully on the head. And, somehow, the name seemed right.

● ● ●

A Brat at Night

One day, Karen arrived home to discover Jose asleep on her bed with Brat curled into a tight ball at his side. "I didn't feel well enough to go to school," he explained. "My stomach feels terrible."

Jose slept all afternoon. He rose briefly for dinner, but by then, tiny red spots had begun to appear on his arms and chest. "I think you have the measles," Karen told her son. "Get some sleep, and first thing in the morning I'll take you to the doctor."

Jose went to his room and closed the door. He knew from experience that if he left it open, Brat would keep him awake half the night wanting to play. He was too tired and achy for that.

It was about two o'clock in the morning when Karen was awakened by the strangest sensation. Something wet and scratchy was pressing against her eyelid. It was Brat's tongue. She reached out, only to feel a furry tail slipping through her fingers as Brat jumped off the bed.

"Not now," Karen muttered groggily, then drifted quickly back to sleep. A few minutes later, Brat licked her eyelids once more, then sprang off the bed and scampered into the hallway. Again, Karen brushed it off.

The third time it happened, Karen came grudgingly awake. "I suppose you want to be fed," she guessed, climbing slowly out of bed and slipping into a robe. Brat raced to the bedroom doorway and glanced back to make sure Karen was still following her. Then, in a flash, she disappeared down the darkened hallway.

When Karen reached the hallway, she heard strange bumping noises coming from Jose's bedroom. "It sounds like he's rearranging furniture," she thought curiously.

And then she spotted Brat. The kitten wasn't waiting at her food dish in the kitchen. She was huddled at Jose's door, scratching frantically, trying to get inside.

Karen opened Jose's bedroom door, but Brat did not race inside. Instead, the kitten sat down on the carpet and peered anxiously up at Karen. And then Karen glanced into the room.

"Oh my God!" she gasped, horror-struck by what she saw.

Jose was writhing on the floor in convulsions, his hands clawing at empty air and his eyes rolled far back in their sockets. He'd fallen off his bed, and his body was scraped and cut from bumping into furniture. "Help!" Karen called to her husband, Bill. "Call an ambulance! Something is terribly wrong with Jose!"

At the hospital, the news was grim. Jose had bacterial meningitis. "It's very serious," the doctor told Karen. "It's a good thing you were able to get him here so quickly. He never would have survived until morning."

Karen thought about the kitten that had been so determined to wake her up. "Somehow, Brat knew that Jose was in trouble," she marveled.

● ● ●

A Brat No Longer

Cats may not have the same reputation for sensing danger and saving lives as Lassie or Rin Tin Tin, but according to Noelle DeMasi, D.V.M., a veterinarian in Larchmont, New York, it's not always for lack of trying.

"Cats can not only be amazingly sensitive to their owners' moods, they're often also quite tuned in to their physical ailments and can even sense danger," she says. Dr. DeMasi has several elderly clients whose cats refuse to leave their laps if they're feeling poorly.

She also tells of one cat who stopped eating for no apparent reason. A little investigatory work revealed that the cat's owner had recently been diagnosed with cancer and was contemplating suicide. Only after the owner sought counseling for depression did his cat's appetite return.

Fortunately, when Brat sensed that something was wrong with Jose, she was able to communicate her concerns to Karen. "I think God sent Brat to us for a reason," Karen says.

Jose spent the next 5 days in a deep coma. Then, slowly, his condition began to improve. Before too long, he was his old self again.

Brat was waiting at the front door when Jose finally came home. She leapt into his arms and nuzzled his neck. "I knew you were the perfect cat for me," Jose said, pressing his cheek against her warm, silken fur. Brat had missed her best friend terribly while he was gone, and she was determined to make up for lost time. During the rest of Jose's convalescence, she rarely left his side.

Karen tried rewarding Brat with different brands of kitty treats and other gourmet delights. But Brat always turned up her nose. Brat, it seems, already had her reward.

"I suppose that when you begin your life in the backseat of an abandoned car, the only treat you really yearn for is a family that's healthy and happy and, of course, always ready to play," Karen says. ✪

chapter twenty-five

The World
through Wild Eyes

*W*hen you bring something wild into your life, you change it. It becomes domesticated. It learns to trust you. It learns to live with you.

But it also changes you.

For example, in the Western states, where cattle graze freely on government land and ranchers gather their herds on horseback, wild mustangs still roam the ranges, fitting in among the other wildlife and livestock.

Centuries ago, broncos and burros escaped from Spanish settlers and made their homes on the ample acres of grazing land, where few predators threatened their survival. Today, their descendants thrive in herds throughout the West.

Most members of the wild herds are protected property of the federal government and remain as range wildlife. But many have become participants in a U.S. Bureau of Land Management adoption program and have been placed on private ranches.

If they receive the right training and find the right home, they will often be better-tempered than domestically bred horses, say wild-horse owners Kate Bremer and Lisa Dines of Nambe, New Mexico. And that's not all that wild horses have to offer. Forever a part of them is the call of the plains and the whispering sounds of the wild.

"When the wind blows, they get all stirred up," says Lisa.

Lisa's red roan, a gelded male, is named Sahwave's Eclipse after a group of mountains near Palomino Valley, Nevada, where he was gathered. "I call him Clippy for short," she says, her hands wandering through his thick black mane. Clippy, a short and muscular mustang, has striking characteristics of the Spanish Colonial riding horse—the first horse introduced to the West.

Having to wait 3 months while Clippy was professionally

trained in the Wild Horse–Inmate Program at a state peni-
tentiary was difficult for Lisa. She anxiously awaited the first
ride on her mustang. Kate experienced much the same feelings as she waited for her red paint, Sahwave's Galaloxy, or
"Lalo" for short.

But the wait for their newfound friends was for a good
reason: Lalo and Clippy were learning how to live with humans.

• • •

The Best Option in a Bad Situation

The U.S. Bureau of Land Management began its adoption program in 1973, as an alternative to thinning out the wild herds
by less pleasant means. The wild horse and burro populations
are always increasing, causing fierce competition among herds
of elk and deer for the scarce grasses growing on arid prairie
land owned by the bureau and the U.S. Forest Service.

To make matters trickier, the land is already vehemently
claimed by ranchers for grazing domestic cattle. The answer
was to find new homes for some of the horses. So the Bureau
of Land Management coupled with the prison system in a
truly unique venture.

Once the wild horses are gathered, they are transferred to
a holding facility operated by the bureau. Kate and Lisa decided that they would choose their horses at the Palomino
Valley holding facility in Nevada. There, they met Clippy and
Lalo for the first time.

"They were totally unbroken," Lisa says. "It was exciting
to watch, but kind of scary, too."

For one veteran of wild-horse gatherings, that excitement
is something that never goes away. Palomino Valley horse
corral manager Sharon Kipping has even adopted several of
her own wild mustangs because of it and trained them herself.

Part of the attraction, she says, is that wild horses tend to develop much stronger bonds with their owners than domestic horses do. Because a wild horse hasn't had much exposure to humans, it is nervous and distrustful of its first contact with them. When someone is able to break through that barrier and gain the confidence of a wild horse, it will bond deeply to that person.

Lalo, Clippy, and the rest of the horses were examined by veterinarians, vaccinated, and treated for injuries and illnesses. Then they began their training at a prison.

• • •

Freedom through Incarceration

Brian Hardin, supervisor of the Colorado Department of Corrections Wild Horse–Inmate Program in Canon City, Colorado, where Kate and Lisa's horses were trained, says that gaining the aforementioned trust is the first hurdle in the breaking of a bronco.

But that's easier said than done, he says. "This is a whole different world, training a wild horse. I go through a lot of inmates to see who is going to make it and who just doesn't have what it takes."

Those who do make it have a special ability to make a horse feel safe and comfortable. "We communicate with the horse on his level. It's all in how you move around the horse and get him to come to you," explains Hardin.

The prisoners who train the horses learn to move slowly and to make sure that the horses don't feel as if they are in any sort of danger. Training the mustangs involves repetition and consistency to keep the trust that was so difficult to win.

The process can be frustrating at times, Hardin admits. Nevertheless, he feels that the program is beneficial not only for the horses and their owners but also for the prisoners who train the animals.

"I've seen a lot of guys gain a lot of self-confidence—and they've earned respect from their peers," says Hardin.

● ● ●

Through Several Continents to Home

When Lalo and Clippy were finally able to join Lisa and Kate, it was a sort of historical homecoming. Even though all of the free-ranging horses in the United States are descended from foreign stock, they thrived here because "there was an ecological niche for horses here," Lisa says.

While conducting research for a wild-horse guidebook that she wrote, Lisa discovered that primitive horses may have originally evolved in North America and traveled across the Bering Straight to Asia and Europe. There, they survived, while herds in North America perished during the last Ice Age.

In the early 1600s, Spanish explorers and settlers in the West reintroduced horses to this continent with their Spanish Colonial breed, a small riding horse that is a mix of the Middle Eastern Arabian horse and the African Barb. Although many mustangs resemble the Spanish Colonial, traces of many breeds can be found among the wild herds of the West because others eventually joined their newly wild brothers.

"Some of these horses aren't the prettiest in the world," Lisa says, "but they need homes. They need to be adopted."

Though both history and humanity were interesting to Lisa and Kate, now that the training was done, they were busy with another priority: riding their wild horses.

"I got on him first thing, just bareback," says Lisa. With Clippy's fine coat in her hands, she finally felt the exhilaration that she had known would come.

Kate was right behind her. In Lalo, she found the unrestrained freedom that can only come with something wild.

Soon, the four friends were traveling throughout New Mexico's countryside. Lalo is a challenge to ride through the Nambe Indian Pueblo near her home, Kate explains, because the terrain is carved with dry riverbeds, or arroyos, to which wild horses are not accustomed. The horses prefer to walk on high ridges, where they can see great distances.

"But I was amazed at how calm he was in the arroyo," Kate says.

Kate and Lisa agree that, like domestic horses, their horses have very distinct personalities. Clippy is a bit more bossy and independent than Lalo. He also spends a lot of time checking out his new surroundings and companions. "He's more curious," says Lisa.

Lalo, on the other hand, is more reserved than Clippy—until he sees that Kate is getting ready for a ride. Then he's immediately raring to go. And Clippy is quick to join him.

For Kate and Lisa, that's how it should be: new friends, open trails, and wild natures. ❂

chapter twenty-six

An Injured Woman's Best Friend

In most families, each person has his or her assigned chores. In households with dogs, the family pet is often no exception.

Perhaps you do a little vacuuming while your pup gathers her squeeze toys and neatly piles them in her favorite hiding place. You might pour the orange juice as she brings in the paper. These are the little acts of kindness and good training that are expected from many dogs.

But they are nowhere near a decent day's work for Mosa.

This warmhearted, 65-pound golden retriever mix shares a home in Orlando, Florida, with Janine and Tim Ose and 10 other dogs and cats. She has a little more on her plate than barking at the occasional nosy neighbor. Mosa has made it her job to pinch-hit on the family caregiving team to help ease Janine's daily struggles.

You see, much of the labor in the Ose household revolves around helping Janine get through the day as she lives with debilitating injuries from a car accident. Tim helps out as much as possible, but when he goes out the door, Janine is pretty much on her own. Or at least that's what she thought.

* * *

Knowing When She's Needed

Janine's troubles began on what started out to be an ordinary day.

"I was sitting in my car, stopped at an intersection. Another car hit me from behind, traveling at about 40 miles an hour," she says. The compact car that she was driving was no match for the large sedan that hit her.

"I knew that I was hurt right away," she remembers. A trip to the hospital revealed that Janine had two herniated disks in her back that were pressing on her sciatic nerve. She also had torn ligaments and damaged disks in her neck.

"I was injured at just the right point so that my back and neck troubles turned into fibromyalgia," she explains. Fibromyalgia is a chronic ailment that shows up as severe pain in the muscles and joints.

Janine soon discovered that her life had changed dramatically. "When something like this happens, everything that you know is gone. I can walk, but I can't lift, bend, or work the way I used to. Dressing myself is difficult, and I need six pain pills a day to keep going," she says.

But the changes in her body were not the only surprise. "As soon as I came home from the hospital, I could see that Mosa could tell that something was different. Instead of jumping on me to greet me, she was gentle," Janine explains.

Then, one day, Tim—who normally works the night shift at a local restaurant—was called in for the day shift. Janine was left alone. "My husband had to help me out of bed and help me do basic things such as tying my shoes or pulling on my pants," she says. "The morning that he was gone, I was on the bed, struggling to sit up and bend forward so that I could pull my slacks up, but I could not get into a sitting position."

Her struggles did not go unnoticed. Mosa jumped onto the bed, sat behind Janine, and pressed her body into Janine's back to act as a support. There she stayed until Janine was able to finish dressing.

At the time, Janine was not particularly shocked by Mosa's behavior. To her, it seemed natural that the former shelter dog, with whom she'd developed an almost instant bond, understood her need for help.

"The day that we went to the pound to get a dog, Mosa and her sister were in a cage with a sign on it saying that the two puppies were skittish and unwilling to come to people," she says. "But I thought that she was pretty, so I knelt by her cage. She came right to me. It was love at first sight."

Mosa's helping hands—or paws—did not stop with supporting Janine's ailing back. "I noticed that she began to lie next to the tub whenever I took a shower. When I tried to leave the tub, she would stand and offer her body as a support for me to lean on, so that I could gain my balance and get out without falling," Janine says.

And when it came to everyday household chores, Mosa put her natural fetching skills to good use. "The other dogs usually pull laundry out of the basket to have something to play with. Mosa actually picks stuff up and drops it *into* the basket," she says. The little trick saves Janine a good deal of bending and reaching.

Mosa, which is short for Mimosa—a Spanish word that can be used as a term of endearment, meaning sweetheart—has never been to an obedience school. She has never been trained to do any of these things. She just started helping out on her own.

Amazingly, when all of the other work is done, Mosa also recognizes Janine's need for peace and quiet. "I sometimes have very severe headaches as a result, I guess, of the neck injuries," she says. "If I have to lie down, Mosa quietly joins me on the bed and keeps the other family pets quiet and away from the bed."

• • •

Of Compassion and Canines

No doubt millions of dog owners would agree that theirs are pets with heart. More than just about any other animal, dogs frequently become emotionally engaged family members.

"In a general sense, what Mosa chose to do is very common for dogs," says Patricia McConnell, Ph.D., a certified applied animal behaviorist and adjunct assistant professor at the University of Wisconsin–Madison. "Dogs are such social creatures that they really stand out among mammals as being very nurturing and caregiving to others in their pack—or, in this case, their human family."

Dr. McConnell suggests that the relatively long periods of parental nurturing and support that dogs receive are likely contributors to Mosa's demeanor as well. "Dogs, like people, have periods where their parents basically teach them caregiving techniques by caring for them," she says.

But even within the realm of expected behavior, Mosa exhibits an unusual gift. "What's truly special about Mosa's story," Dr. McConnell says, "is her almost instant reaction to her owner's injury. Animals generally need to learn that there is a certain type of change. But Mosa showed an enormous amount of insight. That's unusual for a dog."

For Janine, any or all of these explanations may be true. But, to her, the key to her nurturing friend's behavior is as straightforward as the name that Mimosa was given.

"Mosa is my baby," Janine says. "She is just sweet." No Spanish translation required. ❂

chapter twenty-seven

A Hamster against All Odds

*Y*ou've heard of Skippy peanut butter. Maybe you think it's a great spread. Bet you haven't heard of Skippy the hamster, though. And when it comes to spreads, this Skippy's number one.

One of a litter of seven, Skippy was the first to leave the nest. He headed to New York City's Upper East Side after being adopted in March of 1996 by Catherine Kiel, an executive vice president with a major public-relations firm. Skippy quickly acclimated himself to the life of a swank single hamster, spending the weekends in the Hamptons and making frequent trips to Miami, where he now keeps a cage at his winter home with Catherine's mom.

● ● ●

The Making of a Legend

On the job, Catherine oversees major accounts for such well-known brand-name products as Lysol disinfectant, Curad bandages, and Wearever cookware. As a side duty, she also manages the office football pool.

In past years, while the men in the office were studying the spread and debating draft picks to help them make their betting selections, Catherine took a more direct approach. "Instead of picking teams, I'd pick the cities based on whether I liked or disliked a guy who lived there," she explains.

Despite her unorthodox methods, at the end of the 1995–96 season, Catherine had placed third in the overall office standings. "I learned that you don't necessarily have to know a lot about football in order to wager successfully," she says.

The following fall, at the beginning of the 1996–97 NFL season, inspiration struck, and Catherine entered the office pool twice—once for herself and a second time on behalf of her beloved pet hamster, Skippy.

"I'd always known how bright Skippy was. I thought I'd

give him a chance to prove it to the rest of the world," says Catherine.

Catherine cut up sheets of paper that had the football teams' names printed on them. Each week she laid out the pairings on her bedroom floor. Then she put Skippy on the floor between them.

"Whichever team he walked on first or put in his mouth and started nibbling, that was his pick," says Catherine.

Everybody thought it was a great joke. Until the 10th week, when the oddsmaking hamster stomped and nibbled his way to a $42 weekly pool, defeating 20 two-legged competitors with a total of 10 wins—the highest single-week score of the season.

Two weeks later, Skippy did it again. He won a second weekly pot in another landslide victory. The frisky furball took a combined two-game lead over his closest human rival. He was also tied as one of only two players to win two weekly pools.

When the fur had settled, Skippy was the undisputed office champ. With a 133-out-of-240 record, the $4 hamster was now worth $253.40. And this figure didn't include the two $42 weekly pots Skippy had already caged.

Philadelphia Daily News sports columnist Stan Hochman isn't at all surprised by Skippy's predictive powers. "I know one big-city mayor who lets his dog help him make his bets, and I know a radio station where they use a turtle to predict NBA games," he says. "Often these animals do well." According to Hochman, Skippy and his ilk don't outsmart themselves by overthinking or by agonizing over their choices. They just make them. "They don't suffer from what we call paralysis by analysis," he notes.

Of course, as everybody knows, that great big NFL wheel

doesn't stop turning just because it's the end of the regular season. There are still play-off games to play and, ultimately, the Super Bowl.

● ● ●

Skippy Laughs Last

Catherine was in Chicago attending a trade show when one of her clients asked which teams Skippy favored in the upcoming play-offs. But since the office pool had ended with the regular season, Catherine hadn't thought to ask him.

The client was insistent. He hadn't done well betting during the regular season, and he was counting on Skippy's advice to help him stage a postseason comeback.

Catherine, always ready to go the extra mile for a client, telephoned Skippy's hamster sitter and explained the situation. "She thought the whole thing was hilarious," Catherine recalls. The woman couldn't stop giggling as she wrote down the teams' names and cut the paper into bite-size pieces. Skippy, who was sleeping at the time, wasn't nearly as amused. He took a quick nip at his sitter when she collected him from his cage, but in the end he came through like a trooper and made his play-off selections based on taste and stompability.

Skippy's picks? The New England Patriots over the Carolina Panthers. The Green Bay Packers over the Jacksonville Jaguars. Skippy, it would seem, does not like big cats.

Skippy was a winner across the board. So was Catherine's client. "I'm not sure how much he wagered, but he was very happy with Skippy's picks," she says.

As for the Super Bowl that year, "Skippy took New England and 14 points," says Catherine. "He must have figured that either Green Bay wouldn't cover the point spread, or New England might surprise everyone in an upset."

As it turned out, Skippy's prediction was neither right nor wrong. The final score was 35 to 21. Green Bay had matched the spread exactly.

Naturally, it's hard to keep a potential gold mine like Skippy a secret. The week of the Super Bowl, he was interviewed by Jeanne Moos for CNN. He also enjoyed a limo ride to the set of *Live with Regis and Kathie Lee*, where, unfortunately, Skippy's prognosticating prowess did not extend to the game of baseball.

And what does Catherine's family think of her furry friend's fame? "My father thought it was foolish, until I mentioned to him that Skippy was investing his winnings in shares of PETsMART.com." She also told him that Skippy is a date magnet.

Once, during a flight home with a coworker, Catherine asked the attendant if the pilot could announce the Monday-night game score. "I'm tied with her hamster for first place in the office pool," her seatmate said. A businessman in first class overheard the exchange and, intrigued, struck up a conversation with Catherine. He wound up asking her out.

"Hey, you use what you can," quips Catherine. ✪

chapter twenty-eight

Where There's Hope, There's Chance

*J*t's an unusually warm day in February. Hope and Chance have spring fever. The two Great Pyrenees run and chase and nip at each other in the melting snow. Their owner, Darlene Ahlstrom, appears at the sliding glass door, and the two dogs race up the wheelchair ramp. It's time for breakfast—and it's time to get down to the serious business of companionship.

Hope and Chance are important staff members at an adult group home called L'amour et L'abri, which means "love and care" in French. Built in a residential neighborhood in Rochester, Minnesota, the expansive homelike facility offers 24-hour care to elderly and disabled residents who might otherwise be sent to nursing homes or institutions.

"I have a combative 81-year-old resident," says Darlene, offering one example of the canines' work. "But when Hope or Chance is with her, a smile will come to her face, and just like that, she's on a different road. They're really comforting to her."

Seeing Hope and Chance running and sliding on their bellies in the snow, you can scarcely believe that less than 6 months ago they were the ones who were in need of tender loving care.

● ● ●

Starting a New Life

Found in June of 1998 along a Wright County, Minnesota, highway—both underweight, with matted fur and leg injuries that required each to lose a back leg—the 2-year-old dogs had been maltreated by a former owner. Before long, their plight received statewide attention through local media and then spread across the Internet.

Darlene, along with dozens of other would-be owners, wrote letters to the Humane Society of Wright County, hoping for the privilege of taking these dogs in. But Darlene's letter stood out. Here was a place that would offer not only 24-hour companionship but also a purpose for these Great Pyrenees, whose ancient purebred characteristics include loyal companionship, fearless devotion, and faithful guardianship—perfect traits for working with special-needs adults.

"There was an incredible response; everyone wanted to help. Kids even did drawings," says Mary Lotz, administrator of the Humane Society of Wright County in Delano, Minnesota. Lotz and the dogs, named by a fellow humane society employee, met with five final applicants. Darlene, the last to be interviewed, was told that she'd hear the verdict within 4 days. But Lotz was so impressed with Darlene's facility and with her interaction with the dogs that Darlene heard in 3 hours: The dogs were hers.

Five days later, in late September, Hope and Chance moved into Darlene's group home. Still underweight and recovering from their surgeries, the dogs had to learn how to walk on three legs. They got tuckered out early in the evening and turned in around 6:30 each day. And they were still a bit skittish around people. "When we walked toward them, we needed to be careful not to frighten them," Darlene says. But overall, they adapted quickly. "They just knew that no one would hurt them here."

"Dogs crave attention, love, and affection," says Robert K. Anderson, D.V.M., diplomate of the American College of Veterinarian Behaviorists and professor emeritus and director of the Center to Study Human-Animal Relationships of the University of Minnesota Animal Behavior Clinic in Minneapolis–St. Paul. Unlike a human, if a dog is treated cruelly, Dr. Anderson says, he is likely to forgive and forget. If placed with a new owner, a previously maltreated dog may be starved for attention and may be even more eager to please.

That may, in fact, be why Hope and Chance have fared so well with their new human companions. But these dogs offer something else—an understanding of what it's like to be disabled. The residents know it, and the dogs know it. They identify with one another, and it shows in the dogs' work.

• • •

Tending to Their Charges

The two majestic, all-white dogs begin each day by greeting the residents. Then they see several residents to a bus as they head out for a day program.

The rest of the day, these chief morale boosters, part-time therapists, and true friends keep the other residents company by napping next to their wheelchairs and entertaining them with doggie antics. They even accompany them on outings such as checking out nearby Silver Lake to watch Canada geese.

Most important, Hope and Chance instinctively shift their moods to complement their companions. One example: They know how to help a resident with cerebral palsy mellow out when he becomes agitated.

Currently, Darlene's husband, Don, and their grand-daughter, Danielle, take the dogs to obedience classes. Soon the canine pair will begin official therapy-dog classes, al-though they're such naturals that they could probably teach the class themselves. "They give us so much," Darlene says. "These dogs *live* therapy, and they really train themselves."

That's true, says Kathy Gaughan, D.V.M., a veterinarian at the Kansas State University Veterinary Medical Teaching Hospital in Manhattan. The most important qualities of a therapist—love, understanding, and total acceptance—are in-nate in dogs such as Hope and Chance. "They don't judge you because you're incapacitated or frail or unable to move a limb," she says. "They love unconditionally."

"Great Pyrenees dogs are very good therapy dogs," sec-onds Janet Ingram, a rescue coordinator with the Great Pyre-nees Club of America in Midland, Virginia. "They're fairly laid-back; they're calm; they're very tolerant; they have a good temperament. And their size is a plus because, when seated next to someone in a wheelchair, they're big enough that they can be patted and touched."

Darlene set one rule for humans regarding touching Hope and Chance: They must be loved equally. "If you touch one, you touch the other one, too," she says. This was one rule, however, that wasn't difficult to enforce. The dogs are both so lovable that "it's impossible to favor one," says Darlene.

Helping by Being Vulnerable

Meanwhile, Hope and Chance aren't just making a difference in the lives of people; they're helping countless other animals, too. When their story originally became known, money poured into the Humane Society of Wright County.

In all, $17,000 was raised—far more than the $2,500 that their surgeries cost. Today, that money, placed in a special-needs account in honor of Hope and Chance, is helping other pets, paying for surgeries that they otherwise would have to do without.

"Hope and Chance have helped many more animals than themselves," Lotz says. "The bigger picture is what they've done for humane issues. They symbolize what we see every day at the shelter. They brought that message to people for all the other animals out there." ✪

chapter twenty-nine

Diabetes Is No Match for This Cat

*H*ow does a cat see a human? One way is as the keeper of the kibble, the purveyor of Purina. At no time is this more evident than at dinnertime.

Cats can be tenacious when it's time for their supper. When mournful mews and outright meows don't produce the desired result, they'll try other methods to get their owners' attention. Like leaping onto the kitchen counter or getting up close and personal—as though they're more interested in having their ears rubbed than in hearing the wonderful clatter of food hitting the bowl.

Iris Gray's cat, however, is a little different. Iris knows that when Puff starts nudging her hand—or when she jumps on Iris's chest in the middle of the night—she isn't looking for a handout. On the contrary, Puff is reminding Iris that it's time for *her* to eat.

Iris, who lives in Victoria, British Columbia, has diabetes. She needs to watch her glucose (blood sugar) levels closely.

When she starts feeling weak or when her hands start trembling, she pricks her finger to extract a drop of blood, then uses a home testing device to check the amount of glucose in her bloodstream. When her blood sugar level is low, drinking a glass of juice will quickly bring it back to normal.

Iris has had diabetes for most of her life, and she's learned that she has to be sensitive to the warning signs. But Puff, as she discovered, is a lot more sensitive. Not only can Puff sense when Iris's blood sugar level is dropping, but she's also determined to do something about it. And that combination of perception and action may have saved Iris's life.

● ● ●

A Cat Is Watching

One of the greatest dangers of diabetes is that it can gradually damage the small blood vessels that feed the nervous system. This can cause a condition called hypoglycemic unawareness, which makes a person less sensitive to such symptoms as dizziness and shaking. By the time she realizes that

her blood sugar level is dropping, it may already be at dangerously low levels.

During the day, Iris can usually tell when her blood sugar is on the way down and take quick steps to raise it again. But at night, when she's sleeping, her body doesn't always respond to the danger. "If I don't wake up, I could go into convulsions," Iris says. "I could conceivably pass out and never wake up."

One November night, Puff, normally a quiet cat, jumped up and landed squarely on Iris's chest with all of her 8 furry pounds. Half-asleep and bleary-eyed, Iris figured that Puff just wanted some nocturnal attention. But when she reached out to rub the cat's ears, Iris noticed that her hand was shaking uncontrollably.

Iris quickly tested her blood for glucose and was alarmed when the screen flashed 65, which is 20 points below the safe range. Had her blood sugar dipped much lower, she could have lapsed into convulsions, or even a coma. Iris immediately went into the kitchen and got some juice, which raised her blood sugar back into the healthy range. Then she went back to bed, thanking her lucky stars that Puff had happened to want some extra attention at that particular time.

A few weeks later, she felt another late-night thud—and there was Puff, standing on her chest. Once again, Iris realized that her hand was trembling and that she needed to get some extra sugar into her system. Iris was beginning to suspect that this wasn't a coincidence, but it wasn't until Puff had made a half-dozen repeat performances that Iris realized that the cat knew exactly when her blood sugar was dropping—and that she wasn't going to let her human sleep until she took care of it.

"Every time Puff jumped on me, I had low blood sugar," Iris says. "And if she couldn't wake me by jumping on me, she'd meow until I woke up."

Puff doesn't just work the midnight shift, Iris adds. "She doesn't do it too often during the day because normally, when I'm awake, I can tell if I have low blood sugar," says Iris. "But every once in a while, if I'm concentrating on something, she jumps on my lap and gets between me and whatever I'm doing. This is enough to break my concentration and make me realize that my blood sugar is low."

• • •

Super Senses

It's unusual for pets to watch over their owners as closely as Puff does, but her abilities aren't unusual at all. Experts have found that some dogs can predict when their owners are going to have epileptic seizures—probably by smelling changes in body chemistry that are too faint for people to detect. Research has also shown that some pets can identify skin cancers, and others have been trained to recognize signs of pain and to comfort their owners until the pain recedes.

There's a logical explanation for Puff's "cat scans," says Jerry Franz, national vice president of communications at the American Diabetes Association. When the blood sugar levels fluctuate, the body burns fat instead of glucose. This creates waste products called ketones, which change the body's chemistry.

These changes aren't obvious to people, but they may be as clear as Post-it Notes to cats, says Amy Marder, V.M.D., a veterinarian and animal-behavior consultant at Angell Memorial Animal Hospital in Boston, who is also a columnist for *Prevention* magazine and author of *Your Healthy Pet.*

"Animals are very perceptive to physical changes, facial expressions, and emotions," Dr. Marder explains. "It's possible that the cat is picking up on changes in the body that are related to low blood sugar levels."

Iris often tells people about Puff's latest lifesaving exploits, and many of them believe that Puff's ability can't be explained by science alone. There's a good chance that Puff is psychic, they say. How else could she know what's happening in Iris's body before Iris herself does?

• • •

The Healing Bond

Iris isn't sure how Puff knows when she's becoming ill, but she's pretty sure that she knows why the cat takes such an active role in keeping her healthy.

Three years before, Puff was just a skimpy ball of orange fluff living with her littermates in the home of a thrift-shop volunteer. One by one, her brothers and sisters found new homes, but no one picked Puff. One woman showed an interest in adopting the lone kitten but changed her mind at the last minute.

Puff might never have found a home, but at about the same time, Iris, who had just ended a relationship, was looking for a feline companion. Fate brought the two together. Puff immediately moved into Iris's apartment. Soon the meager kitten grew into a long-haired, ocher beauty. Puff was friendly enough with people, but generally she preferred to be looked at, not touched. She spent most of her time perched in high places—in part, Iris suspects, because it allowed her to keep an eye on her territory as well as her owner. Iris did her best to spoil Puff with a steady supply of catnip, kitty treats, and salmon. But she never imagined that Puff would return the favors by taking care of her, too.

The bond between the pair is intense, and Puff is a keen observer, familiar with Iris's every habit, movement, and scent. Iris believes that it's hardly magic that Puff can recognize what's happening in her body even before she does. It's just insight—the kind that only cats have.

New technology will soon make it easier for people with diabetes to detect falling blood sugar levels before they start to cause problems. But the best, fanciest devices will never replace Puff—Iris's meowing miracle worker.

"Some cats bring their people birds and mice," Iris says, but Puff's chosen a different way to express her love. "I'm Puff's human, and I belong to her. I think she's just looking out for me." ❂

chapter thirty

A Tricky Time with Tigers

$\mathcal{J}$t was an extraordinary moment. Workers at the Zoological Society of London were overjoyed the day that Mira, the London Zoo's Sumatran tiger, gave birth. Hari was the first of these rare, endangered cats to be born at the zoo since 1965.

But all was not well. Excitement quickly turned to dismay when the inexperienced mom almost immediately began to reject her infant. Sadly, after only a few hours, mother and cub had to be separated. The blow was even more sorely felt considering the precarious state of Sumatran tigers.

Until recently, all tigers were considered members of the same species, which includes five subspecies—the South China tiger, the Siberian tiger, the Bengal tiger, the Indochinese tiger, and the Sumatran tiger of Hari's ilk. All tigers can interbreed. Unlike other tigers, however, Sumatran tigers have been isolated ever since their native island was cut off from mainland Asia by a rise in the sea level some 12,000 years ago.

Recently, researchers performed DNA testing on blood samples obtained from various captive tigers around the world. The results confirmed a belief long held by many taxonomists, scientists who classify plants and animals.

Because of their extended isolation, Sumatran tigers have evolved at least three unique genetic markers not found in any other tigers. This means that the Sumatran tiger is not just another tiger subspecies. Sumatran tigers are, in fact, a separate and distinct species all on their own.

"These findings add even greater importance to the need to preserve the Sumatran tiger," says George Amato, Ph.D., director of the Science Resource Center at the Wildlife Conservation Society in New York City. "Today, there are only between 500 and 1,000 Sumatran tigers left in the wild. And while we want to maintain all tigers, if we had to prioritize, the Sumatran tiger would receive the highest priority."

And that's exactly what Hari received from London zookeepers.

• • •

A Call for Help

For 10 days, zoo staff member Caroline Connor assumed the role of surrogate tiger mom. She bottle-fed Hari domestic-cat formula every 2 hours. At the end of every day, she snuggled the cub into a box and took him home to her flat in nearby Greenwich. There, cub and Caroline played together on her bed. Later, she tucked him into his box with a hot-water bottle and her favorite plush tiger—which today is a shredded remnant of its former self.

The night that Caroline first brought Hari home, her two house cats ventured near and sniffed curiously at the box.

"They quickly decided that life was far more interesting at the opposite end of the flat," she says.

Hari, named after a river located on the island of Sumatra, became increasingly frisky and playful. But zookeepers worried that the tiger cub was becoming overly familiar with humans. Hari needed a four-footed friend to play with if he was to grow up to become a normal, well-adjusted representative of his species.

Zoological-society officials put out a worldwide call for a suitable tiger companion for Hari. Unfortunately, there were simply no wild-cat cubs of any make or model available to join Hari's play group. And so, London Zoo officials decided to try something a bit unusual. "We got Hari a puppy," explains Caroline.

The tiger's keepers chose a Japanese Akita. These largest of the six Japanese breeds of dogs first became popular in the United States when servicemen carried them home with them from Japan after the Second World War. Akitas are high-energy animals with thick fur and tiny eyes. "All excellent qualities if one is planning to spend any length of time with a spirited tiger cub," observes Caroline.

* * *

A Match Made in London

The first time that Caroline introduced Liffey, the 5-month-old Akita, to her new playmate, the pup bounded over and knocked the tiger cub off his feet. Then, she circled back to Caroline and cocked her head as though to say, "Hey! That was fun! What do we do next?"

For the first few weeks, Liffey and Hari only spent an hour or so per day together, with Caroline serving as both mother and referee. "Occasionally, the pair would fight like, um, er, cats and dogs," she relates. "Initially, Hari could be quite aggressive. It was also a while before Liffey learned that Hari would only tolerate so much pushing around."

Caroline used an old bathrobe, some towels, and cushions to distract the pair whenever their play grew too rough. "Sometimes, they acted just like children," she says. "When one of them would pick up a squeeze toy, almost immediately the other would decide that he simply had to have that very toy for himself."

Despite their differences, it wasn't long before Liffey and Hari were the best of friends. They began spending all day together—chasing one another around their play area or playing tug-of-war with an old towel while zoo visitors unobtrusively watched through the enclosure's several windows.

Later, having played themselves out, the tiger and Akita would curl up together in a corner for a quick catnap. And then, before too long, the fun would start all over again.

• • •

Mementos of Each Other

Unfortunately, not all good relationships last forever. Tiger cubs grow up much more quickly than Akita pups. By the time Hari reached 6½ months of age, he was already so large and strong that zookeepers decided that it was time to separate the tiger cub from his canine companion. They did this gradually, over a period of several weeks, slowly decreasing the amount of time that the two spent playing with one another.

Eventually, Hari was transferred to South Lakes, an award-winning complex for tigers in Dalton-in-Furness, England. There, Hari soon made a new friend, a female Sumatran tiger named Toba. He took with him the gift that Liffey had provided—the ability to associate with other animals.

The tiger couple are enrolled in the European breeding program for Sumatran tigers, which is coordinated by the London Zoo. And while so far there has been no success, zoo officials are hoping to hear the pitter-patter of tiny tiger paws in the very near future.

Back at the London Zoo, Esther Wenman, who is head keeper of the reptile house, took Liffey home to be her pet. Wenman reports that Liffey is a happy, bouncy pup, one who still shows signs of her time with a tiger. While playing with other dogs, she tends to stalk and pounce—little tricks that she picked up from her former feline friend. ❂

chapter thirty-one

A Most Maternal Hen

As almost any working mom can tell you, it can be difficult to find decent day care. Where do you go? Whom can you trust? And what if you're a single mother of four newborns who simply cannot afford to stay home full-time?

Leigh Ann Myers knows what a predicament this can be. But she has also seen an incredible way in which the problem was solved.

Leigh Ann does not have any little ones of her own, but as a third-grade teacher, she spends much of every day educating other mothers' children. She and her husband, Ray, are also the adoptive parents of 120 chickens, nine rabbits, four sheep, a steer, and a turkey.

With that many personalities milling about, the couple rarely knows what to expect. Sure enough, one day, among all the creatures surrounding them, human and animal alike, an amazing thing happened.

An Egg of a Different Sort

On a warm afternoon in April of 1998, Leigh Ann headed across her 3-acre Levasy, Missouri, farm to the henhouse to do her daily egg collection. As she reached into one of the nesting boxes, she was startled to feel a texture that was anything but egglike. It was soft, warm, and furry.

Leigh Ann scooped a tiny creature into her palm and eased it gently from beneath the brood hen. "It was a newborn kitten," she recalls, her voice still filled with awe. "It was so young that its eyes hadn't even opened."

Leigh Ann moved the hen and discovered three more kittens softly purring in the cozy straw nest. She replaced the kitten she was holding. Almost immediately, the hen fluttered back into the nesting box and used her beak to nudge the kittens protectively beneath her wings.

Soon the kittens were kneading her breast with their

paws, looking for food. Unfortunately, given the constraints under which Mother Nature had her operating, all the hen had to offer was a safe place to sleep and an extraordinary amount of patience.

Leigh Ann suspected that the kittens had been abandoned by their mother—she remembered a pregnant tortoiseshell cat that had been hanging around the barn—and she feared that she would have to bottle-feed them in order to keep them alive.

Her worries never came to pass. The next morning, when she returned to the henhouse, the kittens were still curled in the nesting box with the hen, and their bellies were mysteriously plump with milk.

The puzzle was soon solved. Over the next several days, Leigh Ann caught occasional glimpses of the mother cat scampering in and out of the henhouse. Then, one afternoon as she entered the henhouse, she encountered a sight that brought a tear to her eye. The mother cat was lying on her side in the nesting box. As Leigh Ann approached, she could clearly hear the tiny sucking sounds of nursing kittens. "And the whole time, that hen just sat there, cooing contentedly," she says.

When the kittens were done nursing, they scrambled one by one back under the hen's wings. The hen, which Leigh Ann now calls Nanny, clucked and cooed as the mama cat slipped to the floor and disappeared out the henhouse door.

"It's quite remarkable that any mother cat would entrust her kittens to a hen," says Sara Etkin, an animal behaviorist in New Rochelle, New York. Cats are solitary creatures, she adds, and they aren't usually known to engage in surrogate parenting behaviors. "Obviously, however, that mama cat sensed that her litter would be safe with Leigh Ann's hen," she says.

The mother cat and her "sitter" continued their unique day-care arrangement for nearly 3 weeks. Then, one day, three of the kittens were gone. Their mother had moved them to a neighbor's property. A few days later, she moved them again—this time to the Myerses' barn.

But why had the mother cat taken only three of her kittens? The fourth, a gray kitten with tiger stripes, was as fit as the others, so she hadn't abandoned it because of poor health. Could it be that the mother cat had sensed the hen's strong maternal feelings and had decided to repay her kindness and devotion in the only way she knew? Or had the hen been unwilling to relinquish her adopted children, putting up such a squawk that she'd left the cat with little choice but to leave one of her kittens behind? Leigh Ann says she'll never know.

• • •

Hens throughout History

Down through the ages, hens have been considered an archetypal symbol for maternal love and protection. Consider the New Testament passage, Matthew 23:37: "O Jerusalem, Jerusalem, thou that killest the prophets, and stonest them which are sent unto thee, how often would I have gathered thy children together, even as a hen gathereth her chickens under her wings, and ye would not!"

"Hens are among the most maternal of farmyard animals," says Karen Davis, Ph.D., president of United Poultry Concerns, a nonprofit advocacy group for domestic fowl. "It's not uncommon for a mother hen to fight eagles, hawks, and even humans to her death attempting to protect her young."

Occasionally, a brood hen will foster another hen's chicks or even abandoned infants of a different species. Dr. Davis tells of one chicken who adopted a family of orphaned ducks and even coaxed them into the water when it was time for them to learn to swim.

"There's no way we can know whether these hens understood that these were not their babies," she says. "But obviously, in each case, the hens saw something that needed mothering and responded wholeheartedly to that need."

In hens and human moms alike, giving birth stimulates the production of a pituitary hormone called prolactin, which in turn stimulates the production of milk in mammals and triggers a bird's instincts to nurture its young. Often called the mother hormone, prolactin helps to foster the emotional bond that leads many mothers, even adoptive mothers, to devote their lives to their children.

"Increased prolactin levels also inhibit the production of eggs," notes Peter Marler, Ph.D., director of the Center for Animal Behavior at the University of California, Davis. Nanny, always a good layer, produced not a single egg the entire time she was caring for the kittens.

When they were old enough, Leigh Ann found a good home for the three kittens that the mother cat had continued to nurse. She adopted the fourth one herself, named her Munchkin, and weaned her on a mixture of lamb's milk and baby food.

Fittingly, Munchkin soon became best buddies with a lamb named Scamper. Nowadays, the two can often be seen roaming around the Myerses' farm with Munchkin clinging to Scamper's woolly back.

Meanwhile, Nanny is back to laying eggs. But Leigh Ann reaches under her a little more carefully now. Just in case there's a kitten. ❂

chapter thirty-two

Scarlett Saves Her Kittens

*T*he emergency call came through at 6:06 A.M. An abandoned warehouse was on fire in a rundown Brooklyn neighborhood known as East New York.

Thirty firefighters rushed to the scene through a driving
March snowstorm. At the wheel of one of the six fire trucks
was David Giannelli. In his 21 years as a New York City firefighter, David has bravely entered hundreds of burning buildings and saved dozens of lives.

But on this particular morning, David's heroism would not
be called upon. On this particular morning, the job would be
handled quite nicely by a hero of a different variety. A hero
even of a different species.

"The entire warehouse had gone up like a bonfire," says
David, who is a member of Brooklyn Ladder Company 175.
He and his colleagues were already familiar with the building
from previous fire calls.

They knew the interior of the building. They also knew that if someone was trapped inside, it was bad news. The fire was raging so out of control that any rescue attempt would have been exceptionally difficult, if not impossible.

But there *was* a rescue underway. And it was happening right under David's and the other firefighters' noses.

● ● ●

An Introduction to Scarlett

The fire had all but been put out when David heard three faint cries for help. He followed the anguished sounds. They led him straight to a trio of terrified stray kittens cowering on the sidewalk near the neighboring building, not 5 feet from the dying flames. Their fur was scorched and smoky. And they were alone.

David called out for a box. When a police officer gave him one, he nestled the tiny kittens inside it and carried them several yards, out of harm's way. "I'll be back," he promised, and returned to helping with the fire hoses.

But then, a few minutes later, he heard more meows. He searched and searched until finally he spotted two more kittens huddled against a different building across the street. These kittens were also scorched from the flames. They, too, had been left alone.

Ever so gently, David nestled these two kittens into the box alongside their littermates. "There has to be a mother cat somewhere nearby," he thought. Glancing toward the remains of the burned-out warehouse, he murmured, "I hope she got out in time."

While the rest of the fire crew stowed their equipment, David searched for the kittens' mother. He finally found her behind a pile of rubble in an abandoned lot not far from where she had left the second two kittens.

She herself could have escaped the fire easily. But this devoted mother cat had braved the inferno not once but five times in order to rescue her babies and carry them one by one to safety. Then, after ferrying two of them across the street to an even safer place, she had collapsed in pain and exhaustion on her way back for a third.

"My heart dropped when I saw her," David recalls. "She wasn't moving at all, and at first glance I didn't even think she was breathing. Her mouth and face were badly scorched, and the bottoms of her paws were blistered and caked with soot. Her earflaps and whiskers were all but gone. Her fur was so burned that there were large patches of blistered red skin showing through."

The cat let out a soft whimper of pain as the compassionate firefighter scooped her into his arms. "At least she's alive," he thought, carrying her to the box so she could be reunited with her litter.

David still marvels at what happened next. "The kittens started mewing, all excited to see their mama. Only their mama couldn't open her eyes to see them, her lids were so swollen from all the smoke and burn blisters."

And so this brave mother made do as best she could. On legs wobbly from pain and exhaustion, she pressed her nose against each of the kittens in turn and sniffed—identifying and counting. One, two, three, four, five.

Only after she'd finished the head count and satisfied herself that all five of her babies were present and accounted for did she allow herself to collapse inside the box. Whimpering in pain, she arranged her scorched body protectively around her kittens. Then she began purring a weary, guttural purr that seemed to say to her kittens, "It's okay. I think we're safe now."

"It was the most incredible, the most heartwarming thing I've ever seen," says David, who is no stranger to rescuing burned animals. Several years back, this modest firefighter had risked life and limb to retrieve a puppy that someone had left leashed to a post inside another abandoned building that had gone up in flames.

After administering oxygen on the scene, David had carried the moribund mongrel back to the firehouse, where he'd made numerous calls trying, unsuccessfully, to locate a shelter that would agree to help.

He'd all but given up hope when he reached the North Shore Animal League in Port Washington, Long Island. The league readily offered to treat the puppy's burns and subsequently went on to find the pup a good home.

● ● ●

The Long Road to Recovery

The day that he found Scarlett, David needed to make only one phone call to enlist aid for his family of feline refugees. "Bring them to us immediately," a league employee instructed him.

Forty minutes later, when David pulled into the parking lot, he discovered the league's entire medical staff waiting for him outside in the blustery snowstorm. The staff rushed the kittens into the facility's clinic, where they split into two teams led by Bonnie Brown, D.V.M., chief of veterinarian services, and Larry Cohen, D.V.M., the assistant director at that time. Dr. Brown took charge of the kittens, while Dr. Cohen treated their mother, whom a league employee dubbed Scarlett because of the numerous patches of singed, reddened flesh that covered her body from nose to tail.

Scarlett and her kittens were treated for shock, and their wounds were cleaned and dressed. They were given antibiotics to help stave off infections. Then, they were placed inside a special, intensive-care animal cage where league veterinarians could closely monitor oxygen levels, temperature, and humidity.

Sadly, the tiniest kitten did not survive. But Scarlett and her four remaining kittens, which Dr. Cohen estimated were approximately 4 weeks old, responded well to treatment. Indeed, the very next day, when Dr. Cohen placed a dish of food in front of Scarlett, she wolfed it down ravenously, and soon she was back to nursing her purring progeny. After another 2 days, Scarlett even managed to open her still-swollen eyes.

• • •

Scarlett Moves the World

Commenting on Scarlett's act of extraordinary maternal love and bravery, Dr. Cohen observes, "We weren't surprised by what Scarlett's instincts led her to do. But, like everyone else who has heard the tale, we were more than a little impressed." Within days, calls and letters began pouring into the league from around the globe. "I can't recall another case that even comes close to matching the outpouring of public support we received in regard to Scarlett and her kittens," recalls Marge Stein, director of public relations and advertising for the North Shore Animal League.

Scarlett and her kittens spent nearly 4 months recuperating from their injuries. During that time, the animal league received many thousands of letters offering to adopt the now-famous felines. A panel of judges was convened, and every letter was read and judged to find the very best homes possible.

The kittens were adopted in pairs by local Long Island families. And what of Scarlett?

"By the time that Scarlett was ready for adoption, she had become, well, in all honesty, just a little bit spoiled from all the attention," admits Stein. "Besides wanting to find her a very special home, we also felt that she would do best in a home where she was the only pet, so that she would continue to get all of the attention."

The letter that won the judges' hearts came from Manhattan copywriter Karen Wellen. A few months after Karen was involved in a serious auto accident, her beloved 21-year-old cat, Moffitt, had passed away. The accident had also left Karen with lingering back and leg problems.

"The physical and emotional pain I have endured through these years has made me a more compassionate person," Karen wrote. "I vowed that if I ever allowed another cat to enter my life, it would be one with special needs."

Today, Scarlett divides her time between Karen's Manhattan apartment and Karen's parents' Brooklyn townhouse. She still has a few scars on her face and paws, but all of her fur has grown back, and these days this pampered pussycat weighs in at a plump 17 pounds.

"She loves to cuddle and play," Karen says. "She's without a doubt the most lovable cat I've ever known."

Scarlett has experienced the very worst that life has to offer, but through it all, her maternal spirit has remained indomitable.

"It just goes to show that, whatever we face in life, somehow we can overcome it," says Karen. ✪

chapter thirty-three

When Yogi's Not So Cute

Cassie has lots going for her. She has a shiny black-and-white coat, a rock-solid physique, a glow of health, and fiery oak-gold eyes. She has the brains to match her good looks, too. She's easygoing, amazingly trainable, and intuitive to the point that her owner swears that the dog can read her mind.

But when someone sees the 57-pound dog standing toe-to-toe with a 7-foot-tall, 350-pound bear, it's not those other things that stand out. It's her guts.

Cassie is unique among dogs. For starters, she's a Karelian bear dog, one of a breed rarely seen in North America. And she goes through the above-described scene more than 150 times each summer and fall. Why? Because she and her owner, Carrie Hunt, of Heber City, Utah, are on a mission.

It's a mission that involves two sets of historic foes. One set is Karelians and bears. The other is humans and bears. And while contact between these groups once led to injury or death, nowadays everybody is walking away alive.

A Crazy Idea Takes Off

May through November are the months when state, provincial, and national parks in the United States and Canada expend their resources and energy—and sometimes even ammunition—trying to keep wild bears away from people's campsites.

Bears, and their unfortunate interest in coolers and campers, backpacks and tents, are Carrie's and Cassie's area of expertise. As a biologist, Carrie has spent more than 20 years trying to resolve bear conflicts. As a dog born from a historic breed engineered to hunt bears, Cassie is a full partner in Carrie's efforts to keep bears safe by teaching them to steer clear of campsites and other populated areas.

Because of the efforts of both owner and dog over the past few years, scientists and park rangers are finding hope for the first time in decades that bears can be retrained instead of just ignored until they become such threats that they have to be killed.

But the road to this realization has been long and hard. When Carrie first came along with her pretty black-and-white dogs (Cassie has a couple of helpers), many a park official

scoffed at the thought. No way, they said, could her canine team solve the bear problem in places like Yosemite National Park and Glacier National Park.

For starters, it seemed too naïve an idea. Shepherding the bears away with dogs was too simplistic to work.

Second, it seemed to defy the laws of nature: Why should a 700-pound grizzly bear give a hoot about the barking or hassles brought on by a couple of 60-pound dogs? The only way to truly take care of a problem bear, history had proved, was to shoot it.

Last, there was the issue of funding. Who would pay for such a project? Even to those few who thought that the idea had promise, it seemed doomed to fail.

But Carrie was determined that she could pull it off with the right dog. She decided on the Karelian breed because of its history of being bred to hunt bears. Unlike most dogs, at least some members of this breed would be born fearless in the face of the much bigger, intimidating creatures.

Good Karelians were hard to find, though. The breed originates in Russia and Finland and has rarely been exported to North America. Carrie spent years looking at puppies from the few litters of Karelians that were born in her area, without luck.

But then, in 1989, she met 4-week-old Cassie at the home of a breeder in Cody, Wyoming.

"I went and looked at these six puppies, and I knew that I was looking at my dog," says Carrie. "She had a presence. She knew herself, and she knew what she wanted to do. I was torn between Cassie and her sister, who was a cuddler. But I made myself choose her. I knew that she would have what it took."

The Making of a Bear Dog

Together, Carrie and Cassie fumbled through getting to know one another. "There was nobody to teach me what Karelians were like," says Carrie. "They're not like Labs; they're not like heelers. They don't want to suck up to you. They don't live to please you. They do want to work with you, as individuals and independent thinkers." It took her a long time, she says, to just let Cassie be a Karelian.

Karelians possess a unique combination of intelligence, independence, and sensitivity, she explains. "Especially sensitivity. If you're heavy-handed with a Karelian, you'll ruin her," she says. "They are like glass inside."

Soon, the two were as close as a mother bear and her cub. Training was over, and it was time to work. In the years that Carrie and Cassie have been together, Cassie's jobs have been diverse, but her first and favorite job is chasing bears.

Every bear season, the team sets off for Montana, Wyoming, Arizona, Canada—anyplace that has to deal with problem bears. Once they arrive, they begin what amounts to lessons in ursine etiquette for grizzlies and black bears. They rely on the bears' instinctive desire to avoid conflict to teach them to steer clear of campsites and populated areas.

"The dogs are very quick and absolutely fearless," says Carrie. "Cassie can work all day or all night chasing and staving off a bear until she wears him down." And it works.

The scientist and Cassie, and the team of dogs with whom they work, first put themselves between a bear and a campsite. Then, they work at teaching the bear to associate the campsite with unpleasantness—namely barking, snarling, threatening, antagonistic dogs.

"The handler has to set up the lesson for the bear so that his easiest option is to walk away," explains Carrie. "I usually work with three or four handlers and three or four dogs on my team. We always give the bear a way out, a good head start, and we try not to get too close. As soon as the bear starts to do the right thing, we stop all stimuli. The dogs let him walk out of the situation."

● ● ●

The Value of a Bear

In 1997 and 1998, their first 2 years of full-out bear efforts, Carrie and Cassie were able to train more than 100 bears to stay away from campsites. About one-quarter of those were grizzlies. And since only about 1,000 of those bears exist in the contiguous United States, it was a major conservation effort for the species as well as a safety measure for campers.

In one case, at a Yosemite campsite, fewer bear conflicts were reported than had been in any year for the past 4 decades. Not bad numbers for a team whose tactics had been pooh-poohed by critics since day one.

"Cassie has single-handedly changed the way that bears are going to be handled throughout the world," says Carrie admiringly. "Her work has enabled me to prove to the scientific world that bears can be taught, and that bears don't have to be killed. In this case, a dog is *science's* best friend."

Carrie's best canine friend has other roles as well. In the off-season, Cassie has given birth to a litter of puppies every other year since she was 2. In all, there have been 14 babies to raise. Together, she and Carrie train them to run bears.

"I teach the pups obedience," says Carrie, "but Cassie teaches them their work ethic, their focus, their intensity, and their attitude toward life. She shows them how to track. She shows them what I think is important. She's the mother of my team, and she's their teacher, too."

Perhaps it's Cassie's mothering nature that makes teaching schoolchildren about the program her second favorite pastime. "She loves doing tricks for children," says Carrie, "almost as much as chasing bears."

In the skit that the team presents at local schools, Carrie asks Cassie what kind of work she does, and Cassie sits up and begs. "That's right, begging bears!" Carrie exclaims. "And what happens to begging bears who don't leave campers alone?" she asks, then points a finger at Cassie and shoots an imaginary gun. Cassie rolls on her back to play dead.

At the end of each long day, whether she has spent it on the trail or in the halls of local schools and churches, Cassie cuddles up on Carrie's bed for a little hard-earned rest and extra attention.

"Cassie is my hero," says Carrie. "She's also my child, my partner, and my friend. She has earned my greatest admiration. I can't imagine my life without her." ❁

chapter thirty-four

A Prescription for Two

Lisa Conti's home is a shrine to wolves. It's filled with wolf wall hangings, a wolf blanket, wolf statues, wolf coasters, a wolf rug, wolf books, and wolf jigsaw puzzles. Drawings of wolves are even etched on Lisa's T-shirts.

And a few feet away from her lies the closest thing to a real wolf in the whole room: a spaniel–Border collie mix named King.

King begins to bark. He continues as Lisa tries to reassure him. "It's the people next door," she tells him softly. By now, King has jumped to his feet, raising his head up like a sentinel and making all the racket that his small frame can muster. Lisa reaches out to pet him and ruffle his fur. "We're safe," she says, almost delightedly, in that voice that people reserve only for pets and babies. "I'm safe." It's as if she still can't believe it.

"I'm safe because you saved me!"

When Life Wasn't Safe

It's a scene that neither Lisa nor King could have imagined a few years ago. Back then, there were no such safety zones in their lives. There was no comfort. Trust was a thing of the past, an abstract concept.

Both Lisa and King had seen the worst side of human nature, and, to top it all off, most of the world had given up on them.

By the time that she met King in 1995, Lisa Conti had tried everything. She'd been in therapy for years. She'd taken a whole pharmacy's worth of drugs with unpronounceable names. She'd been hospitalized more than 100 times, one of those times for 372 days straight.

But no treatment was strong enough to make her want to leave her house—not even to go to the store, not even to get the mail. She left only to go to her therapy appointments, coming straight back home to a life ruled by fear, depression, and frequent panic attacks that made her feel as if she were dying.

This was not a life that she had chosen for herself. Rather, it simply, tragically, had become that way. Years before, while serving overseas, Lisa and another woman had been raped and burned with cigarettes.

It wasn't until months later that the depression began to sink in. After she finished her tour of duty and returned home on leave, she was hurt again. One day, as she helped her parents build a woodshed, a saw slipped and severed her thumb, which had to be reattached. It was an accident, of course, but Lisa had little emotional strength left to cope with it.

"That was something that shouldn't have happened either," she says. "That really threw me into the depression and the nightmares."

For the next few years, Lisa was often suicidal. She was eventually told that she would never get better. Fearing that her life would be slowly erased, she moved from New York to Maryland, where she hoped to receive better treatment at the Veterans Affairs Medical Center in Baltimore.

Little did she know that her prescription for a normal life would not involve more drugs or more therapy. It would not be filled by traditional psychiatric methods. In fact, it would not be anything that you'd find in a typical doctor's textbook.

Lisa's miracle cure would be something warm, fuzzy, and, at the same time, heartbreaking—a fearful, abused, severely underweight dog whose time was almost up at the local animal shelter.

• • •

Meeting a King

John Butchart, M.D., a psychiatrist at the medical center, says now that it was only a hunch at the time, but that he'd heard stories about service dogs and believed that such a dog might be just the thing for Lisa.

"She'd been on a lot of medication, and we just weren't getting anywhere with it," says Dr. Butchart. "A medication can reduce your anxiety, but it cannot change your view of the world. If you think that the world is a dangerous place, there's no medication that's going to make you think differently."

Dr. Butchart's hunch turned out to be Lisa's lifesaver. King was just what the doctor ordered—and then some. More than just a faithful companion, King has become Lisa's "lifeline to the world," as she likes to say. Now licensed as a guide dog (the state of Maryland has no formal classification for therapy dogs), King accompanies Lisa everywhere. He goes with her to work, to school, and even to Ravens football games. He is her best friend as well as her safety net, alerting her to dangers both real and perceived.

King knows before Lisa does when a panic attack is coming on, and he licks or nudges her hand so that she realizes what's about to happen. Leading her away from stressful situations before she develops a full-blown attack, he does whatever it takes to keep Lisa calm, whether it's wedging himself up next to her or rolling over to show his belly. "He knows that's what I need. I get a lot of comfort from his belly," Lisa says as she turns to pat King.

This kind of human-dog telepathy didn't happen all at once, however. When Lisa met King at the Maryland SPCA, she quickly learned that the world had not been kind to him either. No one was quite certain what had happened to King before he arrived at the shelter, but it took him a month to learn to trust Lisa. (He still won't eat out of metal bowls, which leads Lisa to suspect that he was abused with metal objects earlier in his life.)

In short, King was not the kind of dog for whom it is easy to find a home. Given the choice between a healthy puppy jumping for joy in one kennel and a fearful dog cowering in the back of another kennel nearby, most adopters would choose the former.

But Lisa was not like most adopters. A lifelong dog lover whose family had always adopted dogs from shelters, she needed no more prompting after she heard that the scared, skinny dog with long, black hair was slated for euthanasia that day.

Once home with King, Lisa worked gradually to reduce his fears, letting him build the relationship on his terms. Allowing *him* to decide when to come and sit by her, Lisa melted away his distrust. By the time he was ready for behavior training, King was already extremely sensitive to Lisa's well-being. From there, it was just a matter of polishing.

"We trained the dog so that any time he was under stress, he would come to Lisa," says Jonathan Collins, a dog trainer and professor at Catonsville Community College in Maryland. "Dogs are just as sensitive as human beings. When they're in need, they go to whatever their strongest support system is."

• • •

A Therapeutic Friend

King now shows no signs of being the fearful dog he once was. He runs to greet visitors as they pull into the driveway. He gladly accepts treats from the man who delivers mail to Lisa's office, and he makes the rounds to greet her coworkers every day.

He frequents the dog park, socializing with his doggie friends but still poking his head around trees once in a while to make sure that Lisa is safe. Now, though, King's mere presence makes her feel safe most of the time—or at least safe enough to attend Catonsville Community College, where she studies recreation in the hope of becoming a park ranger, and safe enough to work as a student aide 20 hours a week. Lisa even feels safe enough to live without therapy and medication. King is all the medicine that she needs.

"He just gave me my life back," she says. "I know that even if I have a panic attack, I'm not going to be alone. He's going to be there, and he's going to help me through it. Even if people around me don't understand what's going on, he's there. And focusing on something else outside my body when the panic attacks are going on shortens them."

No one is quite sure what triggers the painful memories that lead to panic attacks, says Dr. Butchart, but people go through the same feelings that they experienced during the original trauma. "They usually only last for 10 minutes or less, but during that time it's very frightening," he says. "And when you look at the whole picture, basically it is the response of somebody who is preparing to either fight or flee."

Usually, such attacks have a domino effect, creating a "chemical cascade" that feeds on itself and does not subside until all the dominoes fall into place, says Dr. Butchart. "King somehow can interrupt that cascade by diverting Lisa's attention. Before it has gone too far, the dog has already indicated to her that everything is safe. And of course, this implies a huge trust in the dog. I think that somebody like Lisa, and others who suffer as she does, can trust a dog better than another person."

* * *

The Return of Safety

The success of relationships such as Lisa's and King's remain relatively obscure and mostly unexplored in scientific literature. Lisa hopes to change all that. In fact, she and another veteran have dreams of starting a foundation that would help veterans and homeless animals start new lives together.

But for now, she and King are so busy with school and work that Lisa barely has time to think. King, especially, has been feeling the pace. In the last couple of years, he has developed epilepsy. Lisa controls it with phenobarbital and lots of haircuts (heat can bring on seizures).

King's condition has made Lisa think. She knows that, one day, King won't be with her any longer. She knows that she will return to the shelter to adopt another dog. But her heart will always be with the one who saved her life.

"There will never be another dog like him. He's my boy," she says as he looks up, sensing that he's being talked about. "Aren't you, buddy? You're my boy." ✪

chapter thirty-five

A Thief among Men

*M*any dogs will go out of their way to show off for the people in their lives. Some may leap to catch Frisbees when playing on the beach. Others may track wild rabbits and bay loudly when the hares are cornered. Yet others might lead lost children home, to the gratitude of parents and owners.

But David Baca's dog, Oliver, is more likely to prey on pocketbooks than on furry forest creatures for a loving pat on the head.

Now, don't get Oliver wrong. He might just aid a stray toddler in his Dixon, New Mexico, neighborhood—but only if he knows that he will be rewarded for the rescue with a greenback or two.

Yes, that's right: Part pug and part Pekingese, and no larger than a chubby Chihuahua, David's dog Oliver is a paper-money bandit.

In Dixon, a rural mountain village that lies on the banks of the Rio Grande in northern New Mexico, David has a small horse ranch that is home to seven dogs—including Oliver and his mate, Mimi, a Pekingese-Chihuahua mix. Mimi, though, is much happier tending the home front than heading out to seek booty with her partner.

While the other dogs at the ranch are dreaming about fox hunts and cattle drives of days gone by, or about digging in the desert for weatherworn bones to add to their hoards, Oliver is most likely dreaming up his next big score.

● ● ●

A History of Larceny

David discovered his pet's affinity for paper money several years ago, when a girlfriend began complaining that she was missing money. For 3 weeks, the woman blamed David for her frequent financial losses. But since he was also short a few $5 bills, the couple couldn't figure out what was happening to all their cash.

Finally, in desperation, they directed their accusations at Oliver. They both knew that it couldn't be the mellow Mimi who was robbing them blind. They set a $10 bill on the coffee table as bait for the thief.

"We watched him one day," David says, "and sure enough, he picked it up." Oliver took the bill and stored it in his favorite spot behind the refrigerator. "We found quite a stash behind the refrigerator. Forty-five dollars or so."

Oliver hasn't stolen *all* of the funds in the stash that he's since moved to David's van. Sometimes he finds a dropped dollar bill lying in a ditch. On other occasions, he uses his crooked smile to swindle money from a stranger— putting on a Humphrey Bogart grin to win over new friends with deep pockets. But regardless of how he gets it, once Oliver comes across some paper currency, he won't let it go.

"He's a character," David says, explaining that his 9-year-old pet is quite popular in New Mexico's taverns, where he often joins David for a frothy beer or two. "Everybody knows him, from Taos to Santa Fe."

But bartenders know to pick up tips quickly when Oliver is around, David jokes, or the dog will snatch them from under their noses.

• • •

A Mild Monetary Mystery

David says that he's still puzzled about how Oliver became a thief and a swindler. "I never taught him that trick. I don't know where he got it from." And David doesn't know how, if Oliver can't steal it, he'll dig it out in more honest fashion.

"One day—it's the honest-to-God truth—he went with me to the post office. He loves to carry mail back home, and he loves to carry wood, too. So there he was, digging in the bushes. He came out with a little green thing all folded up. It was a $20 bill. He was real proud of that."

Oliver's owner was proud, too, but he quickly learned that Oliver wasn't going to hand over his find without a fight. The dog demanded some of the money so he could purchase a package of Vienna sausages, his favorite treat.

David thinks that Oliver's habit of stashing cash may be linked to memories of his younger days, when David was a cattle rancher and always had a couple of extra dollars for Oliver when he passed the grocery store. David would stop down the road at Zeller's General Store, a small grocery in Dixon, give Oliver some money, and send him into the store to buy his sausages. Store clerks who knew Oliver gave him Vienna sausages in exchange for his mouthful of green paper money.

But that didn't last long. Eventually, times got tough at the small ranch, David says. He sold his cattle, and money was tight. "Every time Oliver wanted to stop at the store, I'd say, 'We don't have any money,' and I guess he took it seriously."

Oliver's veterinarian, Jane Salsbury, D.V.M., agrees that Oliver probably *does* remember the wealth of Vienna sausages he had in the past. "I think he does have some sort of understanding" of the connection between paper money and tasty treats, she says, adding that Oliver also may have become attached to David's scent on the money at first, and then just appreciated the human scent that all dollar bills carry.

"I've seen a lot of weird things," says Dr. Salsbury, who serves the mountain region's small and large animals, "but I've never seen this in another dog."

The bond between David and Oliver is quite strong, she says, even though Oliver is not generally friendly with others. In fact, the dog won't hesitate to bite anyone who doesn't heed his polite warning growl. "I can't even cut his toenails without David there," she says—even after 9 years of caring for him.

●　●　●

A Bond beyond Years

David says that he and the "peke-a-pug," as he affectionately calls Oliver, became instant friends on the day that the dog was born. He was actually searching for a pet for his girlfriend when he en countered Oliver's pregnant mother. "And strangely enough, that same day when I went and met her, Oliver was born. He was only as big as his head is now. I think he bonded to me at that same time. After that, he wouldn't go to anybody but me."

Anybody except for his mate, Mimi, of course, and the occasional tawdry poodle.

Oliver has been a busy dog since he moved to David's ranch in Dixon. Back when there were still cattle grazing on the land, he would follow David through the daily routine of feeding horses and riding the range. "He's pretty helpful," David says. "He used to herd cattle when he was young. But now, he's lazy. I have to push him out of bed in the morning."

Once he's awake, though, Oliver likes to work, hauling wood and watching over the horses. Although he's the smallest of David's dogs, Oliver is the leader of the seven-dog pack at the ranch.

And he's a lot stronger than he looks, David says, recalling a time when he was out rounding up cattle with Oliver during a snowstorm. The peke-a-pug got stuck in a snowdrift, but he didn't let that slow him down. He climbed out of one drift and bounded into the next, never losing sight of the frightened cattle.

Now, David and Oliver spend their spare time fishing for German brown trout in the rivers and streams of northern New Mexico. With the Rio Grande running right in front of their home, they don't have far to go for a good catch. The two also enjoy jogging together in the morning and taking evening hikes.

Sometimes, Oliver likes to visit his many offspring who still live around Dixon. At last count, there was Pancho and Pedro, Chula, Zelda, Otto, Gulliver, and Melvin.

"Oliver messed around with a poodle," David explains. "Her name was Fifi, and their kids are the ugliest dogs you've ever seen."

Oliver, offended by the insults to his offspring, scrunches his jaw into a pout. But it doesn't last long. David hands him a dollar bill. "Give a smile," David says. "Give a big smile, Oliver."

And Oliver breaks into his best Bogey grin. ✪

chapter thirty-six

The Miracle
of a Mother's Love

*N*ancy Abecassis is a longtime cat lover. She has eight cats of her own, and, for more than a year, she was coordinator of a South Florida Humane Society animal foster-care program. During that time, she placed sick and injured strays in foster homes until they were well enough to be put up for adoption.

Today, Nancy owns and operates Pet Nanny, an in-home pet-sitting service. She's also the president of Cat Rescue, a Broward County, Florida, rescue league that finds homes for 75 or more strays every month by featuring them at area pet supermarkets.

Over the years, Nancy has helped to arrange the adoption of thousands of homeless kittens and cats. But there was one very special feline adoption that Nancy will never forget.

The tale began late one night when a neighbor called Nancy from a local college. "There's a stray cat wandering around the parking lot, and you can tell just from looking at her that she has no home," the woman said. "She's right here now, rubbing against my legs. She's so sweet. Should I bring her to you?"

The cat was a lovable Russian Blue that Nancy decided to call Smokey. Nancy took Smokey to the vet for spaying and to treat a neck abscess. Then she called upon one of her many volunteers to provide foster care for the convalescing cat until it was her turn to be adopted.

A month passed. Then one weekend, when Smokey's foster mom was going out of town, she asked Nancy whether she would mind keeping the affectionate feline for a few days. Nancy readily agreed.

Later that same night, Nancy received a phone call from a woman frantic with worry. "I found this tiny kitten in my backyard bushes, and I can't find the mother anywhere. The poor thing can't be more than a few days old. It looks half-starved."

Nancy advised the woman to obtain some kitten milk re-placement and to try hand-feeding the kitten. "I've never done anything like that before," the woman anxiously replied. "If I bring the kitten over, can you show me how?"

● ● ●

Smokey to the Rescue

An hour later, the woman arrived at Nancy's home carrying a male kitten with black-and-white tuxedo markings, nestled in-side a tattered cardboard box. She set the box on the floor, and the next thing Nancy knew, Smokey had roused herself from a deep nap, padded across the room, and climbed inside the box with the pitifully mewing baby kitten.

Smokey began licking the kitten. Plaintive mews turned to soft purrs as the mouse-size creature nuzzled against Smokey's fur and began kneading his tiny paws against her belly.

"Smokey and the kitten seem to have taken to one another," Nancy told the woman. "I suppose you'd best leave him here with me."

By the time that the woman had gone, the kitten was diligently trying to nurse on one of Smokey's teats. "I'm sure that that's quite comforting, but I think that right now what you really need most is a bit of nourishment," Nancy said to the kitten.

Nancy held the kitten in one hand and a bottle of kitten formula in the other. But the kitten would have none of it. He squirmed and yowled until finally Nancy had no choice but to put him back into the box with Smokey. "You'll get hungry enough eventually," Nancy said, and she decided to wait the kitten out.

But the next day, the kitten still refused the bottle. Despite all of her coaxing, he spit out every drop of formula that Nancy managed to get into his tiny mouth.

And then suddenly Nancy felt a sharp pain. A disapproving Smokey had nipped her in the ankle. "Okay, okay. You guys win," Nancy surrendered, placing the kitten back into the box with Smokey. Immediately, the kitten snuggled up and started nursing. "You can't be getting anything," Nancy said. "Smokey was spayed a month ago."

But as the days passed, the kitten continued to refuse the bottle in favor of Smokey. And incredibly, he didn't appear to be suffering. On the contrary, he was looking stronger and healthier by the day. "Could it be?" Nancy wondered.

Nancy telephoned two vets, but they both agreed: "It's impossible for a cat to nurse an adopted kitten a month after she's been spayed." But soon, the truth was obvious to anyone who cared to look at Smokey's swollen underbelly. Somehow, a full 4 weeks after she had been spayed, Smokey had begun producing milk for her adopted kitten.

And the kitten was lapping it up. "He was a real mama's boy," says Nancy. "He'd lie there in that box all day long nursing. And Smokey seemed so contented. Most of the time, you'd find her giving the kitten a bath or else just lying there with her arm draped protectively over his body."

The kitten nursed so much that Nancy began calling him Tubby. "He got so roly-poly that he looked like a land turtle," she recalls with a laugh. "His belly was so swollen with milk that his legs splayed sideways. That kitten didn't walk across the room; he swam."

• • •

Just Short of a Miracle

According to Patricia Forsythe, D.V.M., a veterinarian in Fort Lauderdale, "Female cats have frequently been known to bond with adoptive kittens, and they often are able to feed them if they've recently been moms naturally. But I've never heard of a cat who began lactating 4 weeks after being spayed, as apparently Smokey did."

Dr. Forsythe offers one possible partial explanation for Smokey's maternal prowess. "In mammals, milk production is regulated by a number of different sex hormones, most notably by a pituitary hormone known as prolactin," she explains.

"Smokey's reproductive organs were removed when she was spayed, so there could have been only trace levels of most sex hormones in her bloodstream a full month later. But the surgery did not affect Smokey's pituitary's ability to produce prolactin," adds Dr. Forsythe. Suckling by infant mammals is known to increase prolactin levels in lactating females. Sometimes it even happens with nonlactating adoptive mothers such as Smokey.

But how did Smokey manage to nurse Tubby without the many other sex hormones essential to milk production? Obviously, Smokey cared for Tubby as if he were her own. Could this be just another case of a mother's love overcoming insurmountable obstacles?

Tubby would probably say yes. If he weren't too busy feeding. ✪

Mind Drifter

GENRE: SCIENCE FICTION

What would it be like to travel into the minds and imaginations of others? Eighth-grader Syah Walker knows exactly what it's like because, as a peer counselor at Emdaria North Middle School, she does just that. Using the high-tech MindLink machine, Syah "Drifts" from physical reality into the minds of troubled students who need her help. Inside the students' minds, she battles alongside them to fight the monstrous mental constructs created by their own fears and anxieties. Along the way, Syah also guides students on a personal journey to break through their inner struggles. Readers will relate to many common middle school issues presented in this highly imaginative and genre-bending sci-fi series. See a video interview with the author and discover more titles in the series when you scan the book with the free Capstone 4D augmented reality app.

		GRL	LEXILE	PRINT
NEW	Dream Monsters: A 4D Book ©19			978-1-4965-5896-1
NEW	Enemy Mind: A 4D Book ©19			978-1-4965-5898-5
NEW	Reject Rebound: A 4D Book ©19			978-1-4965-5899-2
NEW	Wicked Stepsister: A 4D Book ©19			978-1-4965-5897-8

By Gina Kammer •
 1/4" x 7 1/4" • Pages: 128

Set of 4 Print Books: $79.96 ($106.60 List)
978-1-4965-5908-1 SCAN TO CART

...cover: **$19.99** ($26.65 List)

SCIFINITY

MIND DRIFTER

Mind Drifter is published by
Stone Arch Books, A Capstone Imprint
1710 Roe Crest Drive
North Mankato, Minnesota 56003
www.mycapstone.com

Library of Congress Cataloging-in-Publication Data
Names: Kammer, Gina, author. | Demaret, David, illustrator.
Title: Dream monsters : a 4D book / by Gina Kammer ; illustrated by David Demaret and Chris Chalik.
Description: North Mankato, Minnesota : Stone Arch Books, [2018] | Series: Sci-finity. Mind drifter |
    "Download the Capstone 4D app to access a variety of bonus content"—Publisher.
Identifiers: LCCN 2018005699 (print) | LCCN 2018009712 (ebook) | ISBN 9781496559005
    (eBook PDF) | ISBN 9781496558961 (hardcover)
Subjects: LCSH: Peer counseling of students—Juvenile fiction. | Anxiety disorders—Juvenile fiction. |
    Paranoia—Juvenile fiction. | Adolescent psychology—Juvenile fiction. | Mental health—Juvenile
    fiction. | Middle schools—Juvenile fiction. | Science fiction. | CYAC: Science fiction. | Peer counseling—
    Fiction. | Anxiety disorders—Fiction. | Paranoia—Fiction. | Psychology—Fiction. | Mental health—
    Fiction. | Middle schools—Fiction. | Schools—Fiction. | LCGFT: Science fiction.
Classification: LCC PZ7.1.K217 (ebook) | LCC PZ7.1.K217 Dr 2018 (print) | DDC 813.6 [Fic]—dc23
LC record available at https://lccn.loc.gov/2018005699

Summary: As a peer counselor at Emdaria North Middle School, Syah Walker believes that Aman,
    a new boy at school, needs her help. During an emergency MindLink session she drifts into his
    mind and finds that he suffers from severe anxiety and fear of failure. Aman's internal mental
    constructs are a complex blend of secret societies, conspiracies, and threatening monsters that
    Syah must help Aman overcome if she is to help him deal with his struggles in the real world.

Editor: Aaron J. Sautter
Designer: Hilary Wacholz
Production Specialist: Kathy McColley

Printed and bound Canada.
PA020

Download the Capstone 4D app!

- Ask an adult to download the Capstone 4D app.

- Scan the cover and stars inside the book for additional content.

When you scan a spread, you'll find
fun extra stuff to go with this book!
You can also find these things
on the web at www.capstone4D.com
using the password: dream.58961

DREAM MONSTERS

A 4D BOOK

BY GINA KAMMER

COVER ILLUSTRATION BY
DAVID DEMARET

INTERIOR ILLUSTRATIONS BY
CHRIS CHALIK

STONE ARCH BOOKS
a capstone imprint

THE DREAM

Syah had the same dream again. It began as it always did. After finishing her personality skills test on the last day of seventh grade, she watched the screen of her test pad for the results. Syah crossed her fingers, hoping she would get the student helper role she wanted most for the 2310 school year. More than anything, she wanted to be the student artist and make fun designs for the school during her eighth-grade year.

But Syah's test pad flashed a different student helper title on the screen . . . Syah Walker, Student Counselor. Syah stared at it in shock. Student counselors had the hardest job of all. They were the Mind Drifters, as the strange peer counselors were sometimes called.

The dream then zoomed forward. The school counselor, Ms. Moller, was marching Syah down the hall. Eighth grade had just started, and all the student helpers were training for their new roles.

"I have so much to teach you," Ms. Moller said, waving open the door panels to the counselor's office. "But we don't have much time. There's a boy who needs our help. However, it's hard for him to trust anyone. We hope you can help him understand that we're his friends." Ms. Moller flashed her key card to a panel by another door and it slid open.

As they walked into the room's bright light, Ms. Moller put on a white lab coat and moved toward a shiny metal machine in the middle of the room. Red, green, and blue buttons flashed and beeped on it. The machine was hooked up between two narrow tables with thin cushions. Syah knew they were the beds that the student counselor and the student needing help would lie down on. The beds didn't look very comfortable to Syah.

"This is the school's MindLink lab," Ms. Moller explained. "It's where we'll do most of our work." She walked to the machine and had Syah follow. "This is the machine that lets us link our minds with the minds of our patients. Have you ever had a counseling session?"

Syah silently shook her head. She knew many kids went to the counselor for all sorts of reasons. But she had never been in the counselor's office or the lab.

"That's all right," Ms. Moller smiled. "According to your test, you'll pick it all up very quickly."

Ms. Moller picked up the white wires that were plugged into the MindLink machine. They had clear, round, rubbery pads on the ends. They looked a little like the suction cups that would stick to windows.

"First, we place these on your temples." Ms. Moller said, turning to Syah. But then she stopped and laughed at Syah's worried expression. "Don't worry, they don't hurt at all! They just link you and your patient to the machine. It's like dreaming, but we call it *drifting*. You drift from this reality into the other person's *mindscape*."

At that moment, Syah's dream went fuzzy. It jumped ahead again to when a boy was brought into the MindLink lab. He was Syah's first assignment.

Ms. Moller had them lie down on the tables. As she placed the cold round pads on Syah's temples, Syah peeked over at the boy. His name was Joden Ferro.

He looked terrified as Ms. Moller calmly hooked him up with the wires too.

Joden had stopped coming to school and wouldn't talk to anyone. Syah had no idea how she could help him. Even after everything Ms. Moller had taught her, Syah didn't know what to do for this boy.

"It's all right," Ms. Moller told him. "This is Syah's first time with the MindLink machine too. If anything goes wrong, Syah will use a passphrase to signal me. This red button will flash, and I'll turn the machine off."

Joden saw Syah watching him and looked away quickly. Syah swallowed hard and tried to relax.

"Okay, we're all set," Ms. Moller said. "Ready to link in three . . . two . . . one . . ." Then she hit a button on the machine. Suddenly Syah felt dizzy. It was like she was falling down and falling asleep at the same time, but she couldn't pull herself out of it.

Syah opened her eyes and gasped. She sat up straight and saw she was still in her bedroom at home. The dream was over. Syah took a deep breath and looked out her wide, oval window. The sun peeked over the city's tall spires and buildings. It was almost time for another day of school and working in the MindLink lab.

CHAPTER

1

Syah — Science class, Emdaria North Middle School

Syah squirmed in her desk. Science class was just beginning, but she was feeling impatient. She had received good news and could hardly contain her excitement. Syah pulled up the pass Ms. Moller had sent on her tablet again . . .

Permission is granted for Syah Walker to attend Psychology Club Workshop with Dr. Gail Gables. Board the 1145 train direct to Emdaria North Secondary School.

Syah had to tell someone the good news. She opened the message feature on her tablet and began typing a note to her friend Joden.

SYAH: Remember that workshop with Dr. Gail Gables I told you about? I get to go! She's only THE most famous psychologist from the MindLink Institute. My sister's friend says we'll be doing the "Psychology ABCs Workshop." Dr. Gables will go through the different issues Drifters often face when helping people through the MindLink machine. I guess we're starting with anxiety. I seriously can't wait. But I have to get through science class first. :^(

JODEN: I think you'll survive. The workshop doesn't sound that fun anyway. Science is WAY better. At least I get to do all sorts of crazy experiments today at the science museum. You should see these labs. So AWESOME!

Syah remembered that Joden was on a field trip with his science class. She rolled her eyes and typed a reply.

SYAH: Yeah, right. Whatever. You're already like a mad scientist anyway. I'd rather watch MindLink sessions and learn from the great Dr. Gail Gables! But . . . I'm the only middle schooler going. What if the high schoolers just ignore me? Or won't let me participate? I really want to show them what I can do so I can join the psychology club.

JODEN: Well your sister's friend is going, right?

SYAH: Yeah, Reiko. She's a student counselor for tenth grade. She's always really nice to me . . . I guess it'll be fine.

JODEN: See? No problem. OK, gotta go! Good luck!

SYAH: Thanks.

Syah quickly set down her tablet as the teacher, Mr. Mercier, started class. She didn't think she'd be able to pay attention to the day's lesson. However, when Mr. Mercier invited a new student to the front of the room, it sparked Syah's curiosity.

"Class," said Mr. Mercier, "we have a new student starting with us. Aman, tell us a little about yourself."

The boy ran a hand through his dark, tousled hair and bit his lip lightly. "Yeah. Sure thing. So, I'm Aman Razim," he said cooly. "I'm from Lahren City—and no, you haven't heard of it." He smiled, and the class laughed. "It's on the other side of the continent . . . and in the middle of nowhere. And now I'm here, where my mom's company is setting up headquarters." Mr. Mercier thanked Aman and directed him to take his seat.

Syah snuck a look at the new kid as he sat down. He noticed her gaze and, biting his lip again, casually looked away. Syah was impressed. She couldn't believe how carefree Aman seemed. He slouched in his seat and propped up his tablet. Not nervous at all.

Syah would have been terrified of switching to a completely new school in the middle of the year. But Aman appeared super calm. And smart, apparently. He answered all of Mr. Mercier's questions about green-dome botany even though the class was at the end of the unit. Even Syah couldn't answer some of the more basic questions without looking them up.

Still, in spite of his apparent calmness, Syah suspected that Aman wasn't as relaxed as he seemed. His eyes looked puffy and tired, and he kept nibbling on his lower lip. She guessed his big move probably would have drained anyone.

When their teacher wrapped up the class a little early, Syah caught up with Aman before he put away his tablet. "Hey," she greeted him. "I'm Syah Walker."

"Aman," he replied, looking up. "But I guess you already knew that." He gave her a half smile.

"So, Lahren City. What's it like where you're from?"

Aman took a deep breath. "Nothing like Emdaria City, that's for sure. It's tiny. No huge spires or all these moving walkways. My school didn't even have a robotics class, so that's new for me."

Syah raised her eyebrows. "Wow. Sounds like it really is different. So you said you moved here because of your mom's job? What does she do?"

"She's a scientist," Aman said. "She started a company that develops better green-dome growing methods. I kind of know all about this stuff." He waved to the classroom in general.

"Oh! It makes sense now how you could answer every question on your first day!" Syah exclaimed. "For a while I thought I must have *really* been spacing out during this unit. I guess I have some studying to do.

"How about the rest of your family?" Syah continued casually. "What does your dad do? Any brothers or sisters?"

"No brothers or sisters, I'm an only child. And my dad, he's . . . not around anymore." Aman shrugged, pulling in his bottom lip with his teeth.

Syah felt she was missing something about Aman. He seemed a little uneasy talking about his family.

"Oh, okay. So, your mom's a scientist," Syah continued quickly, hoping to put him at ease. "And I'd guess she's a good one since she's moving here."

Aman nodded.

"Is that what you want to do then? Be a scientist, I mean."

Aman hesitated. "Maybe. Well, probably not, actually. I like science, but I like it more as part of the science fiction stories I write."

"Oh, cool. I love sci-fi," Syah grinned, excited. "Have you written many stories?"

Aman acted a little embarrassed but smiled. "A few. I mainly just mess around with some story ideas. But I think it would be fun to be a full-time writer."

Syah jumped in. "Yeah! If you like it, you should go for it. Tell me one of your ideas! If you don't mind, that is."

Aman's embarrassed smile was replaced with a look of surprise at Syah's interest. "Well, I guess I've had this historical idea," he replied. "It's sort of a Victorian mystery, kind of like those old-time sci-fi stories by Mary Shelley and Jules Verne."

"Oooh . . . that sounds like it could be a lot of fun. Do you think you'd want it illustrated? You know, I do some drawing sometimes." Syah turned her tablet to show Aman her science class doodles. He seemed impressed, even though Syah had just been passing the time. "Let me know if you need an illustrator!"

Aman gave Syah a genuine smile. "That would be great! I'll send you some ideas, and maybe you can help me figure out how things should look." Syah was eager to see his ideas. She felt like Aman could possibly be a new friend. They seemed to have similar interests.

"Here," Syah said, picking up his tablet. She added her name to his list of contacts. Then she saw the time on the screen above the classroom door. "Oh! Sorry. I've gotta run!"

Aman watched, confused, as Syah rushed through the open classroom door. "Message me!" she called back to him from the hallway. Then she headed off to catch her train.

• • •

Aman — Cafeteria, Emdaria North Middle School

Aman scanned the lunchroom with his tray, looking for a place to sit. He felt frustrated that something so

simple was the hardest part of his day. He bit his lip and turned to the other side of the cafeteria. No one would look at him. He imagined standing there holding his tray forever, and no one ever waving him over. A stubborn part of him was almost tempted to do just that.

Aman wished Syah were there. At least then he'd feel like he knew someone, even a little bit. Syah had made him feel better. She seemed to like old science fiction stories like he did. But he didn't know where she had rushed off to so fast instead of going to lunch.

Aman stared at the mystery mush on his tray, feeling queasy. He groaned and decided he'd have to make the first move. He'd have to put up the cool attitude again just so the other students might accept him.

He randomly chose a nearby table with a group of laughing boys. Aman strode up to the table and took a seat. Their conversation stopped instantly.

"Okay if I join you?" he asked, trying to sound casual, as if he didn't really care either way. The tone must have worked. The others seemed to relax. Some shrugged. Some gave him a half nod.

"We were just talking about the new parkour arena. Have you checked it out yet?" a blond boy asked.

Aman didn't even know what *parkour* meant. His stomach churned uncomfortably. He didn't really know how to respond but tried to play it cool anyway. He shrugged and commented, "I haven't really had time yet." Then he chewed on his lip while he waited to see how the other boys responded.

They all nodded as if that made sense and began talking about it again. Aman heard their words, but they didn't mean anything to him. He pushed the sludge around on his tray, trying to think of something he could add to the conversation. But no words would come, and Aman soon felt like an outsider.

There's so much to learn . . . so many new things to get used to, Aman thought to himself. *This is a shiny new city with new people . . . but no real friends.*

As Aman's thoughts swirled in his mind, he began feeling a little hot and dizzy. He closed his eyes and tried to calm himself down. If the other students saw how strange he was feeling, it would only make things worse.

Aman had to get away. He swallowed the muck without tasting it, stood up, and gave the table a quick wave. The other boys didn't seem to care. Aman put away his tray and left the lunchroom. He found a quiet spot on a back stairway where he could sit and be alone. It would be a relief to stop trying to impress everyone for a few minutes.

He took out his tablet and started a message to one of his old friends. He started and restarted his message several times before he gave up. How could he explain how different everything was? His old friends might understand how different Emdaria City was, but they didn't have to live there. Or eat the weird food. Or listen to classmates talk about a sport they didn't even know existed.

Remembering his old friends made Aman's chest tighten and brought tears to his eyes. He didn't want to be caught crying. Then he'd never make new friends.

Aman stood up and took a deep breath. He ran a hand through his hair and told himself none of his crazy thoughts mattered. He had to shrug it off and play it cool. If he wanted his classmates to like him, he'd have to avoid making anyone uncomfortable.

CHAPTER

2

Aman — Razim residence, Spire #132, Emdaria City

Aman rubbed his eyes as he stumbled around the strange "perfect posture" kitchen chairs. Just like everything else in Emdaria City, even the furniture seemed too complex and sleek at the same time. The Razims' new spire apartment came fully furnished. His mom hadn't wanted to move their old furniture across the continent, so almost everything was new. In some ways, that was a good thing—Aman wasn't constantly reminded of his old home. But all the newness still felt a little overwhelming.

"Ready for another day?" Aman's mom asked, setting a plate of toast and fruit in front of him. She had been really peppy since they'd arrived in Emdaria. Aman knew she loved her work, and he wanted to feel happy for her. He tried to give her a smile before biting into a plum.

"Now that your first day is out of the way, do you know what you'd like to be involved in at school?" his mom asked. "Maybe a science club? I bet Emdaria North has much better equipment than Lahren City School. To use real, professional technology for once must be so exciting for you!"

"Yeah," Aman said around a mouthful of toast. "It's really great. Um, I already knew everything in my science class so far."

"Ooh, that's great! You'll do really well here. I just know it! You'll have so many more opportunities." His mom clapped her hands in excitement. Aman went along with it all. He knew his news about science class would make her happy. She'd always wanted him to be a scientist like her.

"Well, I'm off. Big plans to go over today to get headquarters up and running. Are you all right getting to the train station on your own?" she asked, worried.

"I'll be fine, Mom," Aman reassured her. He nearly flipped over his lightweight chair as he got up to give her a hug.

The apartment doors whooshed closed behind her. Alone, Aman wandered over to the huge oval window to peer down on the city. He would never get used to how high up their apartment was in Spire #132. They were nearly on the top floor! Even so, hover cars whizzed by the window as they cruised toward the business sector. A giant, clear tube wound around the spires, and Aman caught a glimpse of a mag-train rushing through one. The train's electromagnets sent it hurtling so fast it was only a blur. Lahren City had mag-trains too. However, they were ancient and clumsy compared to Emdaria's sleek bullet-like transports.

Aman knew his mom was right. Emdaria *was* exciting. But it was a lot to take in. The move had happened so suddenly. He hadn't had time to really say goodbye to his old home and friends.

Aman's eyes drooped as he looked out over the cityscape. He shook his head and smacked his cheeks, trying to wake himself up. He had tried so hard to sleep. Yet his brain had spent another night spinning in circles . . . trying to catch up with all the recent changes in his life. Every time Aman had nearly dropped off, he would lurch awake again with fists full of blankets and breathing fast. He blamed his lack of sleep for the recent tightening sensations in his chest and throat.

Abruptly, the apartment doors whooshed open again. Aman spun from the window in a slight panic, but it was only the spire's cleaning bot. A blue light on its smooth, dome-shaped head blinked before it scanned the apartment. A low hum started up as the robot's vacuum base buzzed over the floor. As it moved along, the robot snaked flexible arms out of its many compartments, wielding dusters and polishers of every kind. Aman didn't think he'd ever be used to all the robots in Emdaria's spires. Lahren City had its own robots, of course. But there weren't nearly as many models as Emdaria City boasted.

Aman knew he needed to get going if the cleaning bot was already working. His mom had scheduled it to arrive after they would both be out. The cleaning bot's sensors spotted Aman, and it made an irritated beep. "Okay! Okay! I'm going," Aman told it as he got out of its way. He rubbed his eyes again and grabbed his bag.

As soon as Aman arrived at school, the little energy he had left drained completely. All the strange faces and confusing halls seemed to surround him in a fog. He couldn't bring himself to repeat the previous day. The thought of trying to find his way around all over again made his stomach hurt.

Aman wished he could've stayed home and worked on his story instead. He had spent some time the night before working on it in his head. Ideas for steam-powered robots and mysterious characters bounced around in his brain. He even wrote some notes that he wanted to give to Syah for her illustrations. He had hoped that thinking about his story would distract him enough so he could get some sleep. It hadn't helped.

By the time science class started, Aman felt he might collapse. He sank into an empty desk and took out his tablet. He stared at Mr. Mercier, but nothing made sense. The new science unit sounded like a lot of gibberish. Yet all the other students around him seemed to get what was going on. The boy on his right kept typing notes into his tablet. He must've understood all the new terms the teacher kept using. Aman felt his stomach begin to cramp up.

He twisted around to look for Syah. She sat in the next row a few desks behind him. She didn't seem to be paying attention to much of anything. Her hand rested on an old book made out of paper. He had no idea where she'd gotten something like that. Paper books were rare and hard to find. It had the title PRACTICING MINDFULNESS written on it in huge letters. He shook his head. Nothing seemed to make any sense.

"Hey," Aman whispered toward Syah. But she just stared toward the other wall, idly picking at a knot in her long hair. Aman couldn't catch her attention. Frustrated, he turned back to the front.

Suddenly Aman felt terribly lightheaded, and his vision went blurry for a few seconds. He tried to suck in a deep breath, but he couldn't breathe. The tightness in his chest returned with a vengeance, and he felt as if he might faint. He couldn't let that happen. Everyone would think he was a weirdo. Aman didn't know what was happening. He had felt a little queasy all morning, but he had been able to shake that off. This was something else entirely. This time, Aman felt like there was nothing he could do.

His heart beat wildly—uneven and hard in his chest. His tongue and lips started to tingle. His fingers prickled with pain too. Aman grasped the edge of his desk but couldn't seem to get a grip on anything. His vision started to go hazy, and everything seemed to move in slow motion.

Aman tried to get up, but instead he felt himself falling. All he could think was how people would see him lying on the ground helpless—or worse.

Aman couldn't seem to get any air. And his muscles were cramped up so painfully that he couldn't move. As he lay there, he thought he heard Syah's voice calling his name over and over from somewhere far away . . .

• • •

Syah — Science class, Emdaria North Middle School

"Aman! Aman!" Syah called. She watched, helpless, as Aman hyperventilated on the floor. Syah knew about hyperventilating from her workshop with Gail Gables. It happened when people breathed too fast and could cause dizziness and muscle cramps.

Mr. Mercier ran over to help. "We need to get him to control his breathing," Syah told the teacher. Together they took Aman's arms and tried to help him sit up. But his arms had gone rigid, pulling into his body.

"I should call the nurse," Mr. Mercier said, worried. Syah almost nodded in agreement before she realized the real problem. Aman was having a panic attack. It was just like the simulated one she had seen during Dr. Gables' talk on anxiety.

"Wait!" she said. "The nurse won't be much help. This is a panic attack. It's actually mental. We need to get him to Ms. Moller."

Mr. Mercier narrowed his eyes but asked, "Are you sure about that?"

Syah nodded. "Positive. Call her."

"Okay, but I'm calling the nurse too," Mr. Mercier responded. "He may need medical attention."

Mr. Mercier made emergency calls to the counselor and nurse on his tablet. He showed Ms. Moller what was happening, and she confirmed that Syah was correct. She told the teacher that Aman should be brought to her office right away. The nurse agreed and said she would meet them at the counselor's office.

While Mr. Mercier spoke with the other adults, Syah glanced around at the other students. They were all watching with wide eyes. She felt bad for Aman. The stress of going to a new school was clearly a lot harder than he had let on.

"I'm coming too," Syah told Ms. Moller through the videocall. "I met Aman and talked to him for a while yesterday. I think he needs a familiar face."

Ms. Moller nodded from the screen. "I agree. I could use other methods to help him, but you're right. It would be good for him to talk with someone he knows. I'll call his mother and let her know the situation. In the meantime, keep talking to him, Syah. A familiar voice should be helpful for him."

Mr. Mercier and Syah helped get Aman to the counselor's office. "Thank you for helping to bring him here," Ms. Moller said, directing them to the MindLink lab.

They helped Aman lie down on one of the padded tables, then the school nurse checked Aman's vital signs. "He isn't in danger at the moment," she said. "I'll stay and watch for any medical emergencies. However, I agree that Aman's biggest problem right now is mental."

Ms. Moller nodded. "He needs someone he knows to MindLink with him and help calm him down.

"I tried to contact his mother, but I couldn't reach her," Ms. Moller continued. "But I'll keep trying. For now he's obviously too focused on the panic attack and needs help to break out of it."

Ms. Moller turned to Syah. "Syah, since he knows you, you're the best choice right now. He likely won't understand what's happening when he goes into the Link. You'll have to help him understand that he's not in danger. His records show he hasn't had MindLink therapy before. Thankfully, his mother did sign the MindLink permission form when he enrolled in school." Syah nodded and hopped onto the other table.

Ms. Moller gently attached a set of wires to Aman's temples. "I think *serenity* will be a good emergency passphrase. Use it wisely, but if the situation becomes dangerous, say the word. I'll be watching everything closely from here."

Ms. Moller entered the passphrase into the machine. Glancing at Aman, she saw that his quick breathing had slowed and his muscles seemed to relax a little.

Ms. Moller placed another set of wires on Syah's temples. Syah lay back and reached for the pulling current of the Drift, allowing it to sweep her into Aman's mindscape. As it did, she thought about the simulated panic attack from the workshop. But Dr. Gables had clearly never imagined anything quite like Aman's mind . . .

CHAPTER

3

Aman — Dark city street, Aman's mindscape

Aman opened his eyes and guessed that he must have died. Or gone into a coma. Or something equally awful had happened. This place was dark and strange, yet vaguely familiar. Old buildings lined stone streets. They were nothing like Emdaria's great shining spires. Rather, lamps flickered in the windows of structures made of brick and wood.

Aman glanced down and saw that he was dressed in a long brown coat. With shaky fingers, he pulled out a pocket watch that had too many hands and a lot of strange symbols. Heavy boots covered his feet.

He knew none of it was normal, but somehow it didn't feel strange. *I must always dress like this, right?* he thought.

Suddenly a loud hissing and clanking sound made him whirl around. Four monstrous robots stomped onto the street toward Aman. Puffs of steam gushed up from pipes on the robots' backs. Aman knew that shouldn't be right either. Most robots, even in Emdaria City, didn't walk like that. They hovered or rolled on sleek wheels. Yet he felt like he had seen something like these robots before. He just couldn't think why they seemed familiar.

As the robots drew closer, Aman began to feel ill. His head felt kind of fuzzy and stuffed.

Just then a cloaked figure threw open a narrow door in one of the nearby buildings. "Over here, quick!" the figure called. Aman hesitated. But the robots kept stomping closer, and they didn't look like they were friendly. Aman ducked inside the building and the shadowy figure pulled the door shut. "Shh!" the figure insisted, though Aman couldn't see a face.

One of the robots clanked right outside the door. It stopped. Aman's heart beat like crazy. He heard more whirring and clanking. Then the stomping began again, moving away, and Aman let out an explosive breath.

"Whew! That was close," the figure said. The male's voice sounded young. Maybe just a bit older than Aman.

"Who are you? Where are we?" Aman asked.

"Name's Dodger . . . you?" He held out his hand. Aman still couldn't really see his face.

"Aman, but . . . something's happened to me. I don't know what's going on. I was at school—"

"No time," the other boy cut in. "We're out after curfew. We need to get somewhere safe and out of sight of the clunkers."

"The what?" Aman tried to peek out the door, but Dodger pulled him back sharply.

"Clunkers. You know, the steam-engine machines," Dodger said, giving Aman a curious look. "Don't call them that in front of the magistrates though."

Aman nodded dumbly.

Dodger pulled his hood back a bit, revealing a youthful face with the beginnings of a thin beard. "You really *don't* know what's going on, do you?" he asked.

"I don't," Aman rubbed his head. He felt so weird. Everything seemed so unreal, as if he was having an out of body experience or something.

"Well here are the quick and dirty facts," Dodger replied. "One: Don't be caught out after curfew. Two: The magistrates rule everything, and they're strict. The clunkers enforce their rules. They're nasty, so don't cross them. Three: Stick with me, and you'll be fine. I can't say anything more right now, but I've got a group of friends that I think can help you out. They'll get you back to where you belong."

Aman wasn't sure why, but Dodger's presence helped him feel better. His unease and sickness receded a little. He decided to go with Dodger to find his friends.

● ● ●

Syah — Dark city street, Aman's mindscape

Syah appeared on a brick street lined with the strangest old buildings. She soon realized she hadn't entered any ordinary mind. This mindscape made her smile a bit. Syah thought the Victorian-styled surroundings might be from Aman's stories, the way her own mindscape resembled her watercolor sketches.

She began walking over the uneven bricks, but almost tripped. *What am I wearing?* Syah thought abruptly, looking down to see a ruffly shirt and a wide, old-fashioned belt. She kicked short, laced boots out from under frilly, knee-length skirts. She felt her head and found a pair of goggles holding back her hair like a headband. *Huh,* Syah thought. *Is this how Aman sees me? Like one of his characters? Or maybe his panicked mind is just mixing everything up this way, almost like a nightmare.*

And similar to a nightmare, Syah found herself completely alone on the dark street. She couldn't find Aman. The Drift should have brought both of them near the same spot, but Syah's street was empty. *He must be nearby. He couldn't have gotten far,* Syah told herself before she could worry too much.

She jogged through a mix of brick and cobblestone alleys that made no logical sense. She finally came out onto a larger street and saw two figures on the other side. Some sort of large steam-bot was in her way. She wondered if Aman had subconscious defenses set up. Most minds did. People's worries or fears often formed into physical monsters, or constructs, in their mind worlds. Seeing one here didn't surprise Syah, especially knowing how unsettled Aman's mind was. Then one of the figures across the street turned toward her. In the dim light from a gas lamp, Syah saw Aman's face.

"Aman!" she called to him urgently. But he couldn't hear her over the clunking of the steam-bot construct. She tried again with no better luck.

Ms. Moller had told Syah to make sure Aman knew he was safe so he could calm down in the real world. Syah wanted to hurry to Aman before his panic attack could get any worse. He might not know where he was.

Impatient, Syah glanced around for a way to fight the construct between her and Aman. She was getting frustrated. She knew that Ms. Moller would wonder what she was doing when the MindLink machine showed no progress. Plus, Syah remembered watching Reiko go through the simulation perfectly at Dr. Gables' MindLink workshop. Reiko had defeated a construct and finished the mock anxiety

case with ease. Syah wanted to show the psychology club that she was just as good as any high schooler.

Syah's mood brightened when she noticed a metal rod lying in a nearby alley. She ran to grab it, ready to release some of her frustrations in a good MindLink fight. Then she could get to Aman and explain everything. Hefting the smooth rod, Syah sprinted at the steam-bot, feeling a rush of excitement and energy.

CHAPTER

4

Aman — Dark city street, Aman's mindscape

After the big steam-bot stomped away, Aman and
Dodger snuck out of the building where they were
hiding. As they did, they spotted another clunker across
the street. They were both ready to run, but then Aman
saw Syah. He stopped in surprise. *What is* she *doing
here?* Aman wondered. He was glad to see a familiar
face, even though Syah looked different from how she
did at school. She was wearing odd clothing, and her
face was way too fierce.

Syah jabbed a broken metal bar into the joints of the clunker's leg, and it dropped to the ground. Then, jumping on top of the clunker, she wrenched the rod out and stabbed it through the robot's chest. The robot disappeared into thin air, and Syah dropped to the street, landing in a crouch. When she looked up, breathing hard, she spotted Aman. He heard her call out his name as five more clunkers rumbled up the street behind her.

Aman opened his lips to warn her, but a hand clamped over his mouth. "Don't speak to her!" Dodger warned him harshly. Aman's instincts told him to run to Syah's aid as the clunkers moved around her. But the intensity of Dodger's voice made Aman hesitate.

"Don't trust her!" Dodger warned again. "She's clearly in league with the witches . . . or at least under their sorcery. You saw her make a clunker disappear! That's proof right there. She's a witch!"

Aman was very confused. He had liked Syah and didn't think she could be an evil witch. Somehow he knew that witches meant bad news—just as he could sense that the clunkers were dangerous. He didn't understand how he knew *any* of it. Or why it all seemed a little familiar. Yet, everything just felt *off* somehow.

Aman didn't know what to believe. He decided to play it safe. He nodded, and Dodger removed his hand. "Shouldn't we still help her?" Aman asked worriedly. "You said the clunkers are dangerous."

"It won't matter if she's a witch. The clunkers work for them," Dodger explained urgently.

Aman's forehead wrinkled. "But you just said they worked for the magistrates."

"Yep. And the witches control the magistrates. Although the magistrates don't know that. The witches are too sneaky. It's all the same really."

Aman didn't like it, but Dodger had promised to help him. And until he knew what was really going on, he didn't know how to help Syah, or if he could even trust her. He hurried to catch up as Dodger jogged away.

Aman glanced back once to see Syah surrounded by the five clunkers. She was trying to fight her way out, but she had lost her rod somewhere. Aman's stomach sank heavily. He tore his eyes away and turned a corner with Dodger.

Aman followed as Dodger seemed to run through hundreds of different streets and alleys. As they ran, Aman realized there were only about four types of buildings. They kept repeating to make up the rows of structures along the streets. Some had lights, some didn't. Nobody else was outside, and the two boys saw no other clunkers.

Dodger stopped short at an old inn. He led Aman to a side door and knocked out a complex pattern of taps on it. It opened, but no one was there. Dodger grinned back at Aman, and they went in.

"Is this where your friends are?" Aman asked.

Dodger put his finger to his lips. When they reached the end of the long hallway, a hooded figure stepped out of the shadows to block the door.

"Who claims entrance to the old truths?" the figure said in a deep, mysterious voice.

"I, one belonging to the truth, bring one who seeks truth," Dodger said in a formal way.

"This is the point of no return," the hooded figure responded. "Should the truth-seeker enter, he can never return to lies."

"He understands," Dodger said quickly, nodding encouragingly to Aman. He nudged Aman's boot with his own foot.

"Uh, yeah," Aman spoke up. "Right. I understand." It seemed to satisfy the man. He slowly turned his whole body, and the door opened to a warm light.

"Now I can say it!" Dodger said excitedly. "Welcome to the Ancient Order of the Witchless."

* * *

Syah — City street, Aman's mindscape

Okay. Don't panic, Syah thought, spinning in a wary circle as the steam-bots surrounded her. She couldn't squeeze between them to make a quick break for it. *They're just constructs*, Syah told herself. *I've dealt with this sort of thing dozens of times. Nothing new. Aman must have really strong defenses, or crazy paranoia. Who knew?*

She grimaced at the thought of his seemingly carefree attitude at school. *I just have to break down his defenses and get through to him. Then I can tell him what's going on, and we can get to work on his problem.*

Syah tried to think of a plan. As she tried to think of a way to fight five constructs on her own, and without a weapon, the circle closed tighter. The robots' metallic hands reached out and grabbed her arms, pinning her tight. More mechanical hands clamped around her ankles and they lifted Syah off the street.

The robots started moving, carrying Syah to some unknown location. As they clunked along, Syah considered using the emergency passphrase, *serenity*, to end the MindLink session. But she knew Aman needed her help. He was probably feeling lost and scared. Plus, ending the MindLink abruptly, when Aman didn't really know what was happening, could make his panic attack even worse. So Syah stayed calm and didn't fight. It would be better to wait for a chance to escape.

The steam-bots took her to a large mansion on the outskirts of the city. When they arrived women of various ages met them at the gate. The women all wore historical clothing including long skirts and frilly blouses with corsets or bodices. Small hats, each in a different style, were perched atop the women's crazy up-do hairstyles. Their hands were covered with thick black rubber gloves that flared up over their wrists. Many of the women had little corked bottles slung around their necks like necklaces or strung around their skirts like belts. The bottles were of various sizes and shapes and contained different colored liquids.

The circle of steam-bots around Syah parted as the women approached, waving them back. "Who is this little witch?" one woman said, bustling up to Syah. She had bright purple hair and wore a tiny top hat with a feather plume.

"Who are *you*?!" Syah spat back at her. She didn't feel like wasting time with Aman's ridiculous constructs when he needed her help. Yet she was also a bit fascinated. *How can his mental constructs have such unique personalities?* Syah wondered.

Then Syah remembered that Aman was a writer. It made sense that his mind's constructs would have a lot of detail. They were probably based on ideas he'd already created in his imagination. And since this was his mindscape after an emotional event, Syah knew these characters probably wouldn't be very friendly or helpful.

The woman looked insulted at Syah's response. She scoffed, "I, you ungrateful little witch, am the head of this coven house. Elder Adelia Amesbury. And *you* are out past curfew, whoever you are. You're lucky you were brought to us instead of the magistrates! So you *will* mind your tongue!"

The woman waved her hand dismissively, and the clunker released its grip on Syah. She dropped to the paving stones in a heap.

"Now, I'll ask once again, little witch. What shall I call you?" Adelia asked.

Syah ground her teeth and tried to get her legs under her to run. But her muscles were tense and achy, so she tried to stall a bit first. "It doesn't matter who I am. All that matters is that we're in Aman's mind, and he's the only one with true power here. You can go ahead and disappear now, and save me the trouble. You're just a figment of his imagination, and you're wasting my time!"

"Aha! So you're Syah are you?" Adelia sneered. Syah's eyes went wide in shock. She didn't think these constructs would know her name. However, this *was* Aman's mind. Syah guessed it was possible for his constructs to know anything he knew.

"Well, understand this little witch—in here we're as real as you are. I think you'll find we've settled in quite well in this corner of his mind. And I don't think he's done with us yet!" Adelia laughed bitterly. Then she called harshly, "Lucille! Della! Bring her inside to the lab. We've got some work to do!"

CHAPTER

5

Aman — Witchless headquarters, Aman's mindscape

Aman ducked down a stairway past the cloaked man into a large underground room. In the common room he saw tables holding a lot of lamps and delicious smelling food. Strange objects dotted shelves around the room. Several more cloaked men, wearing talismans around their necks, were scattered about.

"So, this is like a secret society?" Aman asked.

Dodger laughed. "*Exactly* like a secret society. And now you're part of it. Well, you will be, after your initiation."

Aman felt concerned, and Dodger noticed. "Hey, it's fine. Only the Order can help you. And the only way to know about the Order is to be a part of it."

"Can they rescue Syah?" Aman asked.

"The witch girl?" Dodger's face grew dark. "Why bother?"

"She's my friend," Aman said sulkily.

"Don't go sayin' that too loud here!" Dodger warned, glancing around. "The society is called 'Witchless' for a reason. It's the only organization that fights against the witches' influence. They don't trust any women, and most women are witches. Sorry to say it, mate, but it sure looks like your friend has turned witch. You're safe here though. You can learn how evil the witches are and what they've done to the city."

Aman backed away. He didn't know what to trust.

"Don't worry," Dodger said in a soothing voice. "If we can prove your friend was just under the witches' power and not one of them, maybe the Order will help."

"Really?" Aman brightened, feeling more hopeful.

"Sure," Dodger said in his carefree way. Aman was jealous of how casual and confident Dodger seemed about everything.

"Witchless!" a commanding voice called out over the murmured conversations. "We have one here who seeks truth and freedom. The newcomer wishes to be a member of the Ancient Order of the Witchless. Prepare the rituals!" Men pushed back chairs and turned down lamps until only orange glows were scattered around the room. The men formed a ring in the open center.

"Come forward," the man from the door commanded Aman. "State your name and desire to join the Witchless."

Aman stepped forward with Dodger hissing instructions behind him. Aman cleared his throat and stated, "Aman Razim . . . wishes to know the truth and find freedom . . . as a Witchless." He repeated each line as Dodger whispered to him what to say. "I vow to keep the trust of the Ancient Order . . . and to never reveal its secrets to another . . . except for those who seek the truth . . . as a Witchless."

The man settled a gold chain over Aman's head. On it hung a circular talisman, a ring with ten tiny points arranged around it like a starburst.

Looking down on Aman, the man said, "Place your right hand over the mark of the Witchless, and repeat after me."

Aman put his palm over the talisman, and it tingled painfully against his skin. He gritted his teeth and repeated the words as the man spoke. "I denounce all connection to witch-kind. I leave behind the lies of the world and take up the truths of the Witchless. I am brother to the Order and am no longer slave to the witches. I swear to keep my oaths to the Ancient Order of the Witchless."

The man turned to face the others. "Do the Witchless accept?"

All the hooded figures around Aman stated in unison, "The Order accepts. Welcome, Brother."

Aman felt a strange sense of belonging. It felt good to be accepted as part of a group. Yet, he wondered what kind of oath he had sworn. Did he just promise not to help Syah? That couldn't be right. Dodger had said the Order could help, didn't he?

The ritual ended, and the hooded figures moved away. Aman pulled his hand off his chest. On his palm, the shape of the talisman was scarred into his skin. He also felt a strange sensation. It was almost as if a string was attached to his palm and was pulling him toward the other Witchless talismans.

• • •

Syah — Witch coven house, Aman's mindscape

Two witches firmly grabbed Syah's arms and hauled
her off the ground with little effort. The gate clanged
shut behind them, and Syah felt a stab of dread. She
was in over her head. Something serious was at work in
Aman's mind. It was much deeper than anything she
had ever encountered before. Syah had a feeling these
so-called *witches* were behind it. She wondered if Aman's
anxiety itself had actually become part of his mindscape.
Perhaps these constructs *were* different from others
Syah had encountered. And that had Syah a bit worried.

The witches tossed Syah into a room that looked
like an old chemistry lab and locked her in. Adelia soon
came in with Lucille, who had wispy white hair, and
Della, with her beehive of green hair. They carried a
tray of various potion bottles. Wispy vapors snaked up
from the mouths of the uncorked bottles, creating a
combination of sharp smells that burned Syah's nose.
She quickly pulled the goggles down to protect her eyes,
though they didn't help her nose.

"These are to ensure your cooperation," Adelia explained, waving at the bottles. "Know that if you don't give us the information we need, we'll use these to get it out of you anyway. But the experience will be much more unpleasant." Syah cringed away from her. Adelia grabbed her arm with gloved fingers and pulled her hand out. She let one tiny drop from a bottle of orange liquid drop onto Syah's bare finger. It burned fiercely, and Syah yelped.

"There, you see?" Adelia said. "Lucille and Della can mix up as much of this as we need." She gestured to the lab equipment and other chemicals running through coils of tubes. Syah thought it looked less like magic, and more like mad science. "You can be sure we won't run out before we're finished with you."

"What in the spires do you want, lady?" Syah spluttered, holding her stinging finger in her other hand.

"It's simple," Adelia said, unconcerned. "Just tell me the phrase that will break the link. Then we're done here. That's it."

"What? I don't know what you mean," Syah said, confused. The witches just shared knowing looks and stayed silent.

Then it dawned on Syah that the witches were talking about the emergency passphrase to end the MindLink session.

Oh no, Syah thought. *Aman must have heard Ms. Moller mention the passphrase back in the lab. He did seem to calm down a little when she programmed it into the MindLink machine.*

Syah didn't know why a construct would want the passphrase, even an intelligent one like Adelia. But then she realized exactly what the witches wanted. They needed *her* to speak the passphrase. She was the only one who could make it work to end the mind link with Aman.

Syah knew that as soon as the phrase slipped from her lips, it would trigger the machine's red, flashing light. Ms. Moller would end the link, forcefully pulling Syah and Aman back to reality before Syah could accomplish anything. Then the witches, steam-bots, and other crazy constructs that represented Aman's fears and worries would remain strong and alive inside his mind.

Why would Aman's mind want to hold on to his fears and worries? Syah wondered. It didn't make sense.

Syah thought about what Dr. Gables had said about the nature of anxiety. Aman's mind wasn't being logical . . . in fact, he *couldn't* be logical. He was stuck in a downward spiral, clinging to his fears and worries so hard that he couldn't help himself.

This is serious, Syah realized. *Aman doesn't know that he's in a MindLink. And I can't break the link because that's exactly what the witches want! They're his fears, and they don't want me to help him. Aman is holding onto his fears with all his might.*

Syah knew that the witches wanted to save themselves by keeping Aman in a state of stress and anxiety. Realizing this made Syah angry. She wasn't about to give up that easily.

Adelia shoved Syah into a plain, wooden chair, and the other two witches held her down. One ripped the goggles down off Syah's eyes. Her eyes immediately began to water from the fumes in the room. Syah pinched her lips tight. She wouldn't let Aman down by giving the witches what they wanted. The witches grinned evilly and came at her with another potion bottle.

CHAPTER

6

Aman — Witchless headquarters, Aman's mindscape

Aman's hand felt tight as he flexed his fingers around the pink starburst scar on his palm.

"You'll get used to it," Dodger told him, nodding to Aman's hand. He brought them both warm mugs of something that tasted like cider.

"What does it do?" Aman didn't know why he didn't say *What does it mean?* like he meant to. He knew the mark felt like more than just a scar.

Dodger leaned in mysteriously. "You'll see." Then he laughed and added, "For one, it's the sign of the

Witchless. It makes you one of us and binds you to the Order. It also helps protect you."

Binds me, Aman grimaced to himself, feeling the invisible tug again. He asked, "Protects me how?"

"From the witches," Dodger said as if it was the most obvious thing ever. "And from their evil *mind sorcery*. They won't be able to persuade you with their words."

"Then isn't the mark a kind of sorcery, too?" Aman wondered aloud. *Sure seems like magic to me*, he thought, rubbing his hand again.

Dodger shook his head. "Of course not!" He sounded offended. "It's all rooted in ancient science. Secret knowledge that has only been passed down through the Order."

"How does it work, then?" Aman asked, not convinced they weren't using magic.

Dodger shrugged. "I don't know. But the Order would never use sorcery like the witches."

"What are all these strange objects and talismans for then?" Aman challenged, indicating the objects around the room.

Dodger pointed to a stick that looked suspiciously like a magic wand. "This one can remove the witches' evil poisons from someone's body when it's waved from head to foot." He then pointed to a cube made of interlocking metal links. "This one is neat. It rises into the air and spins really fast if any witches are near."

"How does it know? Are there electronic sensors or something else that detects magic?" Aman pressed.

Dodger shook his head. "I don't think so. I just know it works."

Aman thought Dodger and the other Witchless were lying about not using magic. "Okay, fine. So can any of these *non-magical* objects help us rescue Syah?" Aman asked.

Dodger frowned for a second, and then whispered, "Well, there is this one thing. There's a chain that's worn like a bracelet. The witches' potions have no effect on the person wearing it. But the High Witchless wears it at all times. He'd never let us use it, though. He's too valuable."

"Well, can't we tell him we just need to borrow it to save someone?" Aman was getting frustrated. He needed whatever help he could get to rescue Syah. In a way, it made him feel good to know someone needed *his* help for a change.

Dodger looked uncertain. Aman tried again. "Isn't that why you brought me here? So we could figure out what's going on? Syah's my best chance to do that, and I think she needs our help."

Dodger finally nodded. "Yeah. Of course," he said lightly. "I'll talk to him."

Aman felt relieved. "Really? Thanks!" Dodger gave him a half smile and walked off.

A while later, the High Witchless stood over Aman's table, pouring the bracelet chain from one palm to the other. At first, Aman got excited. But as soon as he saw the leader's dark expression, he knew he was in trouble.

"Brother Aman Razim," the High Witchless spoke dangerously. "You dare to challenge my authority after we share our secrets with you?"

Aman sank in the hard wood chair, confused and scared. He started feeling panicky.

"Already you break your vow by associating with a witch?" he snarled.

Aman sank down further. Dodger stood a few paces off, looking sheepish. "I'm sorry," Dodger said softly. "I couldn't let you go to the witches. This is for the best."

Aman stared in shock. Dodger had betrayed him!

"Brother Aman Razim, I, High Witchless of the Ancient Order, command that you be taken to our northern outpost, for *safekeeping*. Until you can be properly trained in our ways."

Aman shuddered. He didn't like the sound of that at all. He would never find out what was going on, let alone help Syah—or get home!

Aman grew shaky and hot. He glared at Dodger, his so-called friend. "How could you?" he asked through gritted teeth.

Dodger lowered his eyes and said, "You just can't see it, Aman. Your friend is a *witch*. You saw what she did! Don't you get it? It's no use anyway. She's gone. Don't let her mind games fool you."

Aman refused to believe it. In the hands of the witches, Syah was probably in an even worse situation than he was himself. Aman jumped from his chair and snatched the chain from the High Witchless' hand. He bolted from the room and leaped up the stairs four at a time. Bursting through the door at the top, he stumbled down the hallway and out of the building. He took off down the street and didn't dare to stop running. He'd have to find Syah and help her on his own.

• • •

Syah — Witch coven house, Aman's mindscape

Syah awoke with a stiff neck. She was tied to a chair in the witches' lab. It was dark, and the witches were gone. Syah still felt woozy from the various potions they had used. Some made her brain feel all foggy. Others were painful on her skin. Adelia had been certain that one of the gaseous potions would make Syah talk. But all it had done was make her feel silly, like when she went to the dentist. She stubbornly held onto the secret passphrase.

Syah noted that these so-called "witches" seemed to know a lot about chemistry. They didn't seem to do any actual magic. They also didn't want to harm her too much since they needed her to speak the passphrase. When she finally grew too tired to stay awake, the witches had left her for a time.

Now she needed to figure out how to get out of her mess. As quietly as she could, Syah hopped the chair across the lab to the bench where mysterious new "potions" were brewing. She tried to find something that could free her from the ropes. The only thing she saw that might work was a burner under a large bottle. With hands tied behind her back, Syah tried knocking the wooden chair into the bench near the burner. *If I can nudge the burner closer to the table's edge, maybe I can reach it,* she thought. The chair rammed the bench hard, but the burner didn't budge.

Syah tried again. Harder this time. The bench shook, but she only succeeded in knocking the bottle from its holder over the flame. The glass shattered and the chemical liquid splashed over the table. The flame ignited the liquid, and fire whooshed across the spill.

Syah held in a shriek and tried to hop the chair away. Frantic, she fought against her bonds without success. Other bottles quickly heated and exploded, some throwing even more flammable liquid across the old wood.

Oh, not good! Syah thought, yanking her wrists painfully against the rough ropes. Clouds of smoke and chemical fumes quickly filled the air. Within seconds she got woozy and felt like she might pass out.

Syah slid the chair backward toward the only door in the room. She managed to raise the chair enough to get her hands on the door latch, but, of course, it was

locked. She tried to turn back to face the door, hoping to get a breath of fresh air through the cracks around it. But as she tried to turn, one chair leg caught the rug, tipping Syah onto her side. She landed painfully on her arm and took in a large gasp of toxin-filled air. Her head spun until her vision fuzzed into darkness.

CHAPTER

7

Aman — City street, Aman's mindscape

Aman sprinted down the streets wildly, not caring what direction he was going. He needed to put distance between himself and the Witchless' lies. He could still hear the High Witchless' voice ringing in his ears, "STOP! THIEF!"

As he ran, Aman gripped the special chain so tight that it cut into the raw scar of the Witchless symbol on his palm. He could feel the mark pulling hard on his hand. Hoping to break the link between himself and the

Order, Aman pulled the heavy talisman from around his neck and flung it to the bricks.

Finally, Aman rounded into an alley and threw himself against a wall to catch his breath. He waited and listened. Then he realized something disturbing. He hadn't seen or heard any of the clunkers. Aman didn't think he could count that as luck. Something was going on. Were the Witchless organizing an army against him? Maybe the clunkers *really* worked for the Witchless, and now they'd all be looking for Aman.

Aman tried to think things through. *If the clunkers work for the witches as the Witchless claim, why would Syah have fought one? There's no way she could be a witch. So many lies . . .*

Still, Aman didn't like the thought of dealing with the witches after everything the Witchless had said about them. Yet he knew he *had* to talk to Syah. She was the only person who could help him figure out where he was and what was happening. He bit his lip and peered around the corner into the street. Nothing followed. The street stayed empty.

Aman breathed slowly, trying to calm down. He picked a direction and stuck to it to put more distance between him and the Order. Then he heard the sound of dozens of stomping mechanical feet.

Aman feared the worst, but he had to know what he was up against. He followed the noise, staying hidden in small alleys. Then he saw the clunkers crossing the street several blocks ahead. At least thirty clunkers marched in a line toward something further ahead. Aman followed quietly on a parallel street. He began to see dark clouds billowing into the air. As he drew closer, he saw a flickering glow ahead. The clunkers were all headed in that direction. Aman was surprised; he thought for sure they would be after him.

Aman was close enough to hear shouts of alarm. Then a woman ran right by Aman's alley. She was shouting something about witches burning. *Witches!* he thought. *They must have Syah!*

Aman gripped the chain in his hand tighter and snuck nearer to the clunkers. They were heading to a gate in front of a large, fancy building. It was on fire.

Aman ran to a row of hedges and, staying in their shadows, he rushed for the open gate ahead of the clunkers. The big machines stomped along at a slow pace, and Aman easily beat them in his burst of speed. Once inside the gate, he ducked for cover behind a cluster of trees to figure out what to do next.

The door to the building burst open and several disheveled women poured out. "Coven!" one with sooty, purple hair called out. "Is everyone out?"

"All but the captive, Elder," said one witch with white hair.

"Drat! Without her to say the passphrase, we can't break the link. However," the purple-haired woman said slowly, "I don't think *he* will succeed on his own without her. Perhaps this is for the best!"

"So we leave her, Elder?" a green-haired woman asked hesitantly.

"Yes!" she snapped. "This was her doing, anyway! Let her have what she wanted! She's just getting what she deserves."

Aman listened no longer. The captive had to be Syah. He was certain.

Aman ran around to the back side of the burning building while the witches were busy arguing. He found another entrance and went in. He fastened the chain bracelet to his wrist, then pulled his coat over his head for protection against the heat. The blaze wasn't as strong in the back, so he rushed in and looked around.

He had no idea where to begin looking for Syah. Then he remembered what the witch said: "This was her doing." *If Syah started it, the fire might be worse where she is,* Aman thought. He followed the heat and flames through a corridor. All the doors were open except one on the end. He took a chance and, covering his marked hand with his sleeve, turned the latch. It didn't open. Smoke seeped out around the door.

"Syah! Are you there?! Syah!" he kept calling out her name.

He slammed against the door a few times, and the wood around the latch gave way in splinters. A wave of powerful fumes rolled over Aman. They stung his nostrils and made him nauseated. But then the chain on his wrist glowed briefly and the effects of the fumes disappeared. *Like magic,* Aman grimaced. Yet he was thankful the bracelet had worked against the witches' poisons. Smoke billowed out, and Aman had to blink several times before he saw Syah lying at his feet, tied to a chair.

Aman quickly checked to see if he had anything in his pockets to cut her free. His hand fell on his odd pocket watch, and he wished it had a knife blade. To his surprise, just as he thought it, the blade appeared. It was curved like the pocket watch, as if it could slip inside.

Aman wasted no more time. He unclipped the pocket watch and sliced easily through Syah's ropes. She was completely unconscious the whole time. Aman worked as fast as possible, worried that he was too late.

Once Syah was free, he lifted her up and turned to leave. Her skirts made her heavy, and Aman couldn't shield himself from the heat while he carried her. He stumbled as fast as he could through the hallway toward the back entrance.

Bits of wood and whole beams had begun falling. Aman quickened his step. Bursting through the outer door, he coughed out smoke and took in huge gulps of fresh air. Aman heard people and clunkers heading in his direction, so he ran for a wooded area at the back of the property.

Behind the tree cover, he gently laid Syah on the ground and knelt next to her. He wished he had some water or something to help wake her up. Once again,

just as he wished it, a flask appeared next to his hand.
He opened it and took a sip. It was water. Astonished,
Aman splashed some over Syah's face until she gasped.

"Syah!" Aman said in a harsh whisper. "Thank
goodness! Are you all right?"

Syah stared at him with wide eyes. He gave her
the water to drink, then she spluttered, "Aman? How
did you—"

"I was trying to find you," Aman rushed to
explain. "Then there was all this commotion about
a burning building and witches, and I was worried
that meant you too. And I guess I was right! You were
lucky to be on the floor. Otherwise I think the smoke
and fumes would have gotten to you before I did."

"But the chemicals," Syah frowned, touching the
goggles around her neck. "That's why I passed out.
Why didn't you?"

"That doesn't matter now," Aman said, avoiding
the question. "I'm just glad I found you. Do you know
what's going on?"

Syah nodded, and in a rush she explained,
"Aman, I'm so sorry. You weren't supposed to be on
your own. I lost you somehow after the Drift . . ."

When she saw the confusion on Aman's face, she stopped. "Sorry. I need to explain from the beginning. This is a MindLink session with the MindLink machine. It's used to help people work through their hardest problems. We're in your mindscape. What you think about here becomes real. Even things you don't actively think about, the things in your subconscious mind, those can become real here too. We're really back in the counselor's office. This is all happening in your mind."

Aman stared at her, reeling. So many things made sense all at once. Yet, many other things were even more confusing. "So . . . I didn't die? Or go into some crazy coma or something?"

"Spires, no!" Syah sounded alarmed, propping herself on an elbow. "Oh, this is all my fault. You were having a panic attack during class, and Ms. Moller and I thought this would help. But, Aman, your mind is . . . is . . ." she trailed off as she noticed the orange glow filtering through the branches.

The panic attack, Aman thought, remembering what had really happened. He hadn't been dying. He had just been going crazy, apparently. Aman flushed, realizing how exposed he was with someone seeing inside his mind. It made him nervous. He bit his lip and tried to hide his embarrassment with fake confidence.

"My mind is . . . awesomely imaginative?" he suggested.

Syah blinked. "Well. Yes," she admitted, surprised. "Though I'm no longer sure that's a good thing for a Drifter." She gave him a wry grin, and he felt a little more comfortable.

Their smiles fell as they heard muffled voices at the edge of the trees. Aman could make out the shapes of hooded figures lurking beyond the tree line.

"Uh," Aman said as softly as possible. "I think you need to know something else." The skin tightened on his palm. He felt the familiar pulling sensation. Apparently getting rid of the talisman hadn't worked.

He went on quickly. "I ran away from the Order of the Witchless, and I have something they want." He pointed at the chain on his wrist. Aman chewed his lip nervously and pointed to the figures. "I think they found me." Syah looked confused, but he didn't have time to explain. He grabbed her hand and yanked her up into a run.

They moved deeper into the woods. Shouts followed behind them. "Faster!" Aman hissed, panicking as he glanced back. The confusion fell from Syah's face, replaced by hard determination. She nodded once, and then Aman's hand was yanked forward as Syah shot ahead of him and took the lead.

Aman dared to look back once more, seeing the hooded figures gliding like ghosts around the trees, not far behind. He ran harder, glad to have Syah with him.

CHAPTER

8

Syah — Abandoned shed, Aman's mindscape

A few minutes later the two friends spotted a small wooden shed. Seeing that the door was unlocked, they quickly ducked inside.

"Think . . . we . . . lost them?" Syah asked between panting breaths.

Aman, also panting heavily, peered through the shed's little window. He turned back to Syah and nodded.

"Good!" Syah sank down with her back against the wall, taking a few moments to catch her breath.

"We need some time to talk. We need to get to the bottom of all this . . . stuff . . . going on in your mind. Right now, I can't feel even the slightest trickle of the Drift to get us out of here. Besides, I don't like to give up on my job that easily." Syah scowled, feeling the guilt crash down on her once more for failing Aman so badly.

She studied Aman's face as he chewed on his lower lip. All his confident carelessness was gone. He looked overwhelmed, tired, and scared. Syah's heart went out to him. She *needed* to find a way to help him.

"I think you've been putting on a good show for everyone. Unfortunately, I also think you've held onto your true feelings so tightly that things finally cracked." Syah watched him closely.

Aman nodded and looked toward the ground, ashamed. Tears began to form in the corners of his eyes.

"Aman, it's okay! It's pretty amazing, actually. I can't imagine how you held yourself together for so long. Coming to a new city, going to a new school . . . and in the middle of a school year too. Don't beat yourself up so much. It would be hard for anyone to adjust to such big changes." Syah gave him a small smile, but he didn't look up.

"So there's nothing to worry about, huh?" he said sarcastically. "I should just forget my old life and move on? Sure, no problem. That should be easy."

Syah heard the bitterness in Aman's voice. He was clearly dealing with some strong emotions. She paused, stopping herself from saying something stupid or thoughtless such as, *Just stop worrying, it'll be fine.*

Syah responded carefully instead. "No, you're right. It's easy for someone to say that without really thinking about how another person is feeling. But anxiety doesn't work that way, does it? It's not logical. I can try to say that all of this is in your imagination . . . the witches, this crazy secret Order you mentioned, those scary steam-bot things—"

"The clunkers," Aman cut in. "That's what Dodger called them. Though he wasn't the friend I thought he was."

"What? Oh, sure. That name makes sense," Syah caught on, remembering the figure she had first seen Aman with. "So, yeah . . . those freaky *clunker* things— and bad friends too." She gave Aman a quick grin. The corner of his mouth pulled tight, but he didn't really return her smile.

Syah continued. "These things seem to be bigger than just your imagination. Your mind can't seem to let go of them. If I had to guess, I'd say these things all come from your negative emotions, your worries and fears. Aman, I think it's safe to say you have a really bad case of anxiety."

Aman's brow furrowed deeper and he chewed on his lip again. Syah rushed to reassure him. "It's nothing to be ashamed of, seriously. I just learned this stuff about anxiety in a psychology workshop, and it's very common. In our science class alone there are probably three or four other kids who have some form of anxiety too."

Aman's eyebrows shot up, but he didn't respond. He still looked really worried. Syah changed tactics.

"Look, I don't really know everything about you or your situation. But there are ways to get over anxiety, or at least to help make it better." Despite her hopeful words, Aman didn't seem convinced. She needed him to open up so she could make sure that he knew someone else understood. She took a breath.

"Can you tell me what it feels like?" She waited for him to respond, forcing herself not to fill the silence with more of her rambling.

Aman sighed and slid down the wall next to her.

"It feels like the floor has been ripped out from under me," Aman said. "You know the feeling when you're about to fall asleep, but then you lurch awake, grabbing at your bed? Your stomach sort of drops and your heart races and everything feels out of control."

Syah nodded. "Yeah, I think I get that. It's a pretty scary feeling."

Aman nodded. "Well, imagine feeling that way almost all the time. Especially at night."

"Aman," Syah asked slowly, "have you been getting any sleep?"

Aman shook his head and looked toward the shed's peaked roof. "Not really. Not since before the move. When I found out we were moving, it was all I could think about. I'd stay awake in bed, and all I could think about was everything that would change. I thought it would get better. I'd just have to start living with the changes."

Aman brought his eyes down to meet Syah's. "Then I started thinking about how I don't belong in Emdaria City. Some of it is new and exciting. But I feel like I don't know anything here. And I think I'm going to fail science. My mom never stops talking about how much better the equipment must be than at my old school. And she thinks I have this great opportunity to become a scientist like her. She doesn't get it. I don't even know what's going on in my classes. I'm not making any friends, and I don't know anybody. I'm just a loser here."

Syah wanted to tell him that none of what he said was true, but she knew it wouldn't solve anything. She could see Aman had more than just a general anxiety disorder. He also had a real fear of failure, and it sounded like he didn't want to let his mom down.

"Thanks for telling me what you're feeling. We're going to get you through this. Or at least find a way to help you deal with all of this. That should be enough for me to find the Drift and get us out of here. We can get away from the witches, the Witchless, the clunkers, and the rest of it." Syah smiled. Aman didn't.

"Don't you see? How can I go back after what happened in class? What will everyone think? They probably all think I'm some sort of crazy lunatic!"

Aman looked toward the ground and squeezed his head between his hands. "I think I'll take the witches and the Witchless, and whatever else comes at me here. At least that way no one else has to see how messed up I really am."

Syah felt her own panic rising. The possibility that Aman wouldn't want to get better and face the real world hadn't crossed her mind.

"Aman, we can't stay here. It doesn't work like that. You have to leave here eventually. And don't worry, I'd never tell anyone what you told me. This is all private. I'll keep your secrets." She paused, wondering how she could lighten the mood. "Besides, I'll bet the other kids probably won't even remember what happened in a few days."

"No!" Aman said in panic, standing. "They'd never forget that. That's all they'll remember! I can't face that again."

Syah noticed Aman's hands were shaking as he wiped them on his pants. He began breathing too quickly and became unsteady. *Oh no*, Syah thought, recognizing another panic attack coming on. And this time it was all her fault. She thought quickly through the training from Dr. Gables' workshop. She stood and put her hands on his shoulders.

"Breathe deeply! Slowly," Syah instructed. "The physical stuff that's happening right now—most of it's because of your breathing. You can control it."

Aman's eyes darted around fearfully. "*Just breathe,*" Syah calmly prompted again. "Take a deep breath, hold it for one second, then let it out slowly."

Syah breathed with him, showing him what to do. He followed her lead and he began to calm down. His scared eyes looked down into hers, and she stayed as steady as she could for him.

"Yes, that's it," Syah said in a whisper, feeling awkwardly close to him. "That's exactly right. You have control, Aman. Remember that. Your brain may be throwing your body into overdrive, but you can override it. Take back the control."

Aman nodded shortly, still concentrating on his breathing.

"I think this could work for you," Syah said, trying to get past the awkwardness and backing away a bit. "When you go to bed at night, just try breathing like that for a little while. I think it could help you sleep. And you should practice it so you're ready if you feel an attack coming on."

Aman had calmed down enough to breathe normally again. He sighed, and then he threw his arms around Syah in a hug. "Thank you!" he exclaimed. Syah was too stunned to react.

She finally hugged him back. "Um, sure. No problem. It's my job, after all."

"Seriously," Aman said, releasing Syah, "you don't realize how scary those attacks feel. And at night . . ." he trailed off, shuddering. "I didn't know what was happening to me this whole time."

Syah nodded. "That's why I always think it's better for people to know what they're dealing with. It makes it easier to do something about it."

Aman looked worried again. "But there's so much going on. How can I deal with it all?"

Syah frowned. He was right. And she didn't know the answer. Then she remembered they were in his mindscape. Here they could deal with his issues in a way that was much more visible than in reality.

"Name it," she said abruptly, coming up with an idea.

"Name it? What do you mean?"

"I want you to *name* your anxiety," Syah said seriously.

"What, like a pet?" Aman scoffed.

"Exactly. Isn't that sort of what your anxiety is? You didn't cause them, but you have a lot of worries and fears, and they can get overwhelming. They don't have to be so mysterious though. Mash them together into something and give it a shape. What does it look like? Picture it in your mind. Give it a name so you can separate it from yourself. Then you can command it and learn to control it."

"*Dream Monster,*" Aman whispered. Then he looked at Syah's questioning eyes. "That's what I'm naming it. You're right. My problems are too much to handle separately. But with this name I can remember that they're just in my head. They're part of the crazy dreams I have when I do get any sleep. They're just dream monsters . . . not real."

Syah smiled. Then a shadow fell over her through the dusty shed window. She turned to face the window and dropped her smile. A hulking, hooded figure loomed outside the shed. It wore a talisman of the Witchless. It had a mechanical body like the clunkers. Its hair was the same color of Adelia's, except it squirmed like octopus tentacles. And its face was hideous. The creature was a strange mix of all of Aman's mind constructs. It peered at them through the small window and roared angrily.

"Oh," Syah said in a small voice. Then she turned to Aman. "Right. I told you to picture your fears as a single thing you could fight. Heh. Well, here's your chance."

CHAPTER

9

Aman — Abandoned shed, Aman's mindscape

Aman just stared at Syah. "That's it? *Here's your chance? Are you crazy?*"

"Sorry?" Syah said sheepishly.

Aman began feeling *off* again, like he might faint. Or throw up. Or both.

"Aman," Syah's voice was quick. "Remember your breathing. It's messing up your body's oxygen levels. That's why you're feeling sick. Take control of your breathing. It'll help that feeling settle down."

Aman tried it again. *Breathe in—hold. Breathe out—hold. One. Breathe in—hold. Breathe out—hold. Two.*

After a few more breaths, Aman felt his heartbeat slow down and the feverish heat faded from his body. His hands stopped prickling, and he quickly rubbed his sweaty palms on his pants. *I can control this. I won't let it control me,* he thought.

"Why isn't it attacking?" Aman asked hoarsely.

"Because you've been holding it back—in your mind. Well, *we're* in your mind but . . . ugh, it's complicated. Just know that you're staying in control. That's what's happening." Syah still looked worried.

"I have to go out there and face it, though, don't I?" Aman asked, although it wasn't really a question.

Syah nodded.

"What do I fight it with?"

Syah snorted a laugh. "Hey, this is *your* mind. What do *you* want to fight it with?"

Aman thought for a moment and remembered the metal rod that Syah had defeated a clunker with. "Do spears kill half-mechanical, Witchless, squid-witch monsters?"

Syah snorted again. "Oh, come on! You can think of something way cooler than a spear. Isn't that your specialty as a writer?"

Aman grinned. He thought he certainly could do better. And he was pleased that Syah remembered his love of writing.

He concentrated and a big, bizarre weapon appeared next to the door. It had several brass coils and a round chamber filled with swirling green gas. Syah's smirk split into a wide, amazed grin. Aman picked up the gas blaster and rested it against his shoulder. It was a very satisfying feeling.

"All right, let's take this thing out," he said, taking a big breath and squaring off with the shed door.

"Whoa! Wait a minute! Where's *my* blaster?" Syah asked, sounding offended.

Aman smiled. "Okay. But do you promise to stay my friend after all this?" He imagined another weapon under the window next to Syah.

She grabbed it and hefted it as if she'd always been a make-believe gas blaster expert. "Oh, Aman. You'll wish you could get rid of me that easily!" she smirked. Pulling her goggles over her eyes, she headed for the door.

Aman hurried after, imagining his own pair of goggles on his head. Pulling them in place, he felt confident and in control. It was the first time he'd felt that way in a very long time.

The Dream Monster reacted at once. No sooner were they outside the shed than long purple tentacles whipped out and grabbed the barrel of Aman's blaster.

"Breathe!" Syah reminded him in a shout as she circled around the monster's other side.

Aman did so. He took a deep breath, and as he slowly breathed out, he pulled the weapon's curled trigger to shoot out a spray of acidic gas. The creature squealed and let go of the blaster. It roared even louder. A mechanical leg struck out and knocked Aman off balance. He grunted as he hit the uneven ground, knocking the air out of him.

"Aagghhh!" Syah shrieked as a tentacle wrapped around her waist and lifted her from the ground.

"Syah!" Aman choked, trying to suck in air and shoving himself to his knees. He saw Syah in the monster's grasp. She took aim and sprayed the monster's chest with a vaporous blast from her blaster.

Aman was impressed by Syah's courage . . . until he realized that nothing happened to the creature. The Witchless talisman on the monster's chest glowed brightly and seemed to absorb the toxic gas. None of it touched the creature itself.

Aman groaned and got to his feet, running to Syah. Why had he given the monster so much power? He supposed that was the only way to face his anxiety. He sprayed more gas at the tentacles that were trying to keep him away from Syah. They shrank back each time. At least Aman knew the blasters worked on *something*.

Aman imagined a harpoon-like spear in his path. He picked it up and hurled it at the tentacle holding Syah. He missed, but then he was near enough to use his gas blaster on it.

Syah yelped as the tentacle let her go, and she dropped a few feet to the ground. Then she picked up the fallen spear and hurled it at the monster's mechanical legs. It struck true, and the creature wavered and toppled. It let out a hideous scream and clawed toward Aman.

But Aman was ready. He raised his weapon and tightened his finger on the trigger. *I can beat this thing,* he thought.

"Aman!" a familiar voice suddenly called out.

Glancing over his shoulder, Aman saw Dodger jogging up the street. Aman's teeth clenched.

He knew that Dodger was just another construct now. But he still felt the sting of Dodger's betrayal.

Aman ignored Dodger and put his finger back on the trigger of his blaster. The monster dragged itself forward, beginning to push itself back up. Aman stood firm and released the gas.

"No! You can't!" Dodger shouted. He leapt in front of the Dream Monster. Dodger held out his Witchless talisman before him and the golden symbol drew the gas into itself like a funnel.

Dodger shuddered, looking angry. "What are you doing? Can't you see you're one of us?" Aman watched the Dream Monster still struggling behind Dodger. He raised his weapon again. But Aman could feel a strong tugging on his palm. The pulling made it hard for him to reach the trigger.

"You can feel it!" Dodger exclaimed. "I know it. You have the mark too." Dodger raised his own palm where his scar shone.

Aman glared at Dodger. "I am not one of you," he said defiantly. "I left and threw away the mark of the Witchless!"

Dodger let out a short laugh. "And you think that's

all it takes? The mark is a part of you. You can't just throw it away. You don't get to just leave."

Dodger was right. Aman could feel the pull of the mark drawing him to the Witchless.

Aman glanced over to Syah. She stood in a half crouch, watching. She looked between the two boys and the monster uncertainly.

Aman gave her a quick nod. He needed to deal with Dodger himself. Syah grimaced, but she seemed to understand.

"Leaving was my own choice," Aman said to Dodger, trying to sound more certain than he felt.

Dodger's face darkened, and he shook his head slowly. He pulled his own talisman over his head. In a flicker of hope, Aman thought Dodger might join him.

But then Dodger said dangerously, "So be it."

Before Aman could react, Dodger lunged forward. He dropped the talisman's chain around Aman's neck.

All Aman's courage fled. The weight of the chain overwhelmed him. He knew he had failed.

The Dream Monster roared in triumph and began to pull itself back together. Giving Aman a final look, Dodger vanished.

"Aman!" Syah called. "Look out!"

He turned and came face to face with a clunker. Aman tried to duck, but it caught him and clamped his wrist tight in one move. In its tight grip, Aman dropped his blaster. His heart raced hard. The sound of clunking metal came from all directions. Aman felt dizzy as he struggled to free himself from the clunker's grip.

He heard a rasping voice come from the mutant Dream Monster. "You will answer to the magistrates *now!*" It cackled wildly, but then it stopped abruptly. Aman looked back to see Syah slamming the spear across its evil face. As she raised her arms to strike it again, two more clunkers grabbed her from behind. The spear was ripped from her hands, and she gasped in pain.

"NO!" Aman screamed. They had failed. He had known they would. Why had he dared to hope? How had he even dreamed he could win? It was too much for him. The Dream Monster began to pick itself up. It barely looked dazed.

Then he saw Syah again. She was struggling, but she looked as determined as ever. It was Aman's fault she was stuck in this mess with him. She had only been

trying to help. That made him angry. She didn't deserve
to be trapped here too. He remembered her advice
and started breathing slowly. He got his emotions back
under control . . . sort of. He had stopped the impending
panic attack at least. However, his mind still spiraled
out of control. They had failed. It had all been for
nothing. He fell limp against the clunker that held him.
He was too exhausted to fight it anymore.

The clunker fell in line with the others, and they
began to march off. He heard Syah somewhere in the
line ahead of him, yelling angrily. Aman smiled sadly.
He hoped she could find a way out of his mindscape on
her own. He wasn't sure how the whole MindLink thing
worked. His old school didn't have a machine like that.
But he really hoped she didn't need to rely on him to
escape his insanity.

He shuddered at the idea of meeting the
magistrates. If they were as bad as the Witchless and
the witches, he didn't think he could handle it. He was
terrified of what else his fearful mind had created.

The line of clunkers arrived at an ornate government
building. The steam-bots filed in through enormous
double doors that stretched nearly to the building's flat

roof. They passed through rows of pillars to the end of a long hall. A platform held five evenly spaced high-backed thrones. Seated on the thrones were the thin figures of gray-bearded men. Everything about them was gray. They wore long gray robes and plain gray circlets on their foreheads. The old men looked kingly and powerful.

They watched with empty eyes as Aman and Syah were dumped before them. The clunkers moved back to form a row behind them, blocking any chance of escape.

CHAPTER

Syah — Hall of the Magistrates, Aman's mindscape

"Bow before the magistrates," the five gray men said as one. It sounded like the voices came from everywhere at once. Syah and Aman were on their hands and knees after being dropped by the clunkers. They bowed low, nearly touching their foreheads to the shiny white floor tiles.

"Stand," the strange unison of voices said. Syah got to her feet shakily. Aman remained on the floor.

"C'mon!" Syah hissed out of the corner of her mouth.

"Why bother? What does it matter?" Aman mumbled.

"Because we're in this together," Syah replied. She stepped over and held out her hand. He took it and slowly rose.

"How shall you be judged?" the magistrates said as one. They were looking at Aman. Syah glanced at him worriedly.

Suddenly, a resounding *bang* echoed through the large hall. Syah turned and saw a mob of witches and hooded figures breaking open the doors. Her body tensed. "His *emotions*," Syah breathed. "They're flooding in." Clunkers clanged against one another, forming a solid barrier. Dozens of witches and Witchless had burst inside. They began to overwhelm the clunkers.

Aman laughed, not even noticing the chaos behind him. He answered the magistrates bitterly, "Judged for what? For being forced to move in the middle of the school year? For losing all my old friends? For lying awake each night wishing I could get to sleep?

"What do you want from me?" Aman continued. "I try to act like everything is fine, even when I have no clue what's going on. Then I can't sleep because I feel like I'm making all the wrong decisions. My mom thinks I'm going to be just like her, even though I don't know if I want to be a scientist. I feel awful all the time. I worry about everything. And I'm always on edge. What more do you think you can do to me?"

"Give you logic," came the magistrates' reply.

As Aman considered their response, the clunkers began to fend off the attacking witches and Witchless. Syah saw then how everything was connected. The magistrates *were* logic, Aman's logic. The witches and Witchless were his emotions of worry and fear. Both groups had been lying the whole time. They were actually working together to keep Aman confused and stuck in his negative emotions—his anxiety.

The clunkers were really the link that connected logic and emotion. The witches and Witchless had kept Aman bouncing between bad emotions without letting him see any logic or reason. That is, until the clunkers finally brought Aman and Syah to the magistrates.

Syah opened her mouth to say something, but closed it again. She began to think the magistrates weren't the evil constructs she had expected. They represented Aman's logic and reasoning. Yet something about their offer to Aman bothered her.

"What about emotion?" Syah pulled together enough courage to ask. "Aren't Aman's feelings valid after everything he's gone through?" She had always been taught by Ms. Moller not to discount anyone's feelings. No matter how misguided people could sometimes be, their feelings were still real.

The magistrates' dark eyes fell on Syah, and she shrunk back a little. The gray men's eerie chorus of voices rose, "We are judgment, reason, and logic. We do not feel emotion. Emotion is unreliable. Logic is consistent."

Aman looked curious. "So you can take away my emotions? I won't have to feel all this fear and worry and doubt anymore?"

Just then the witch Adelia and a large Witchless man broke through the line of clunkers. They ran at Syah and Aman. Syah crouched, ready to move.

A murmur ran through the line of magistrates as they turned to one another on their thrones. "Yes. This is reasonable. Your logic is broken by emotion. Removing it will fix the error. The judgement is passed."

Aman sighed in relief. At the same time, Adelia and the Witchless man stumbled and fell, unmoving, almost at Syah's feet.

"No!" Syah cried, realizing what just happened. "Wait! He needs his emotions."

"This does not concern you," the voices of the magistrates said together.

"Oh, but it does," Syah said with certainty. "Aman is here because of me, and I am here to help him." She had to keep them from turning Aman into an empty, emotionless robot.

"The sentence is complete. It is already done," the magistrates said simply.

Syah turned to Aman in horror. His face was completely blank. "Oh, no, no, no!" Syah ran to him. His face showed nothing. He turned to her slowly.

"Aman!" Syah gripped his shoulders. He only blinked at her. "What about friends? What about me? You wanted to be friends after this! Don't you care anymore?"

Aman shrugged. "It doesn't matter. I don't need friends." Syah stared at him, her eyes pleading with him.

Behind the line of clunkers, other witches and Witchless were continuing to collapse. Syah hoped she still had time. Maybe there was some shred of emotion left in Aman. Syah breathed to calm herself. *Okay,* she thought. *If you're all logic, I'll use logic too!*

"You're right," she told Aman, brushing the shoulders of his coat and stepping back. She tried to steady her shaking voice. "Emotion is unreliable, but it's not wrong to have emotion. Sometimes it's helpful. What about gut instincts that logic can't explain? Or when logically, something seems like a perfectly good idea? Maybe someone says all the right words, but your emotion tells you it just doesn't *feel* right. What if it turns out that the person was lying to you? What about things like that? And what purpose does logic serve if there's no emotion left to make someone *want* anything?"

Syah waited. "Your point is logical," the magistrates answered. "Yet what is done is done."

Syah licked her lips, trying not to spin into a panic herself. She turned back to Aman. "Trust me, Aman. You don't want to be an emotionless robot. It may seem a lot easier that way. But shutting down and shutting everything out won't solve anything."

Aman looked at Syah blankly. "This solved everything. I no longer feel fearful or worried. I cannot understand you." Slowly, he removed the Witchless talisman from his neck. He dropped it, but then stared at something on his palm.

"But now you have no emotion!" Syah pleaded. "At first, your focus was so inward you couldn't see beyond your own negative thoughts. Then when you were helping me, you were much more in control. Your emotion, your desire to help someone else, it helped you gain control. You *need* emotion."

As Syah spoke, a new thought occurred to her. "Your emotions need to work with your logic to keep your thoughts from spiraling out of control. Perhaps you just need an outlet for that. Maybe you can use your interests to help others. Even little things can help." Syah hoped something got through to him.

Aman said simply, "I'm not sure it's possible for you to help me." He showed her a strange mark on his palm, the mark of the Witchless. "Your words cannot persuade me."

Syah didn't understand. Did the mark keep him under some Witchless power? She decided she had to try anyway. "Whatever anyone has done to you, you have the power to push past them . . . the Witchless, these magistrates, even me."

The magistrates interrupted. "We do not see the point in this argument. It is not logical. It does not follow what was agreed to. You must be removed."

The magistrates all stood and their gray forms transformed into gaping dark holes of nothingness. The five black holes slowly moved toward Syah. As they moved, everything they touched disappeared, leaving nothing but growing inky black voids.

Syah's mouth fell open in horror. Trembling, Syah turned back to Aman and spoke quickly. "Aman, listen to me! I think you have a terrible fear of failure. It's what you keep saying . . . you're afraid that you won't do well enough. Or that you'll let your mom down and won't meet her expectations. Or that you won't make friends."

Aman gave a small nod, looking down and biting his lip. The familiar action gave Syah a glimmer of hope. She surged on, "Your anxiety problem causes those fears to spin out of control. You think of all the worst possible outcomes. Without logic, there's nothing to keep those thoughts in check."

A spark of understanding seemed to light behind Aman's green eyes. He held Syah's gaze. Encouraged, Syah continued appealing to his sense of logic. "What if your failures are really opportunities? Don't try to live up to what you think your mom wants. Instead, talk to her about what you really enjoy. I bet she'd love to know that you like to write. She probably has great science material you could include in your soon-to-be-famous sci-fi novels." Syah held her breath and waited.

For a small moment, a look of hope flickered across Aman's face.

"Even if you try something and fail," Syah said encouragingly, "failure doesn't always mean negative results. There can be positive outcomes too."

She glanced at the black voids. She found that a few of them were turning gray again, slightly. They were closer, but they had paused.

When Syah turned back to Aman, his face had fallen blank again and he was looking at the mark on his palm. *NO!* Syah screamed to herself. Without thinking, she took his hand, the one with the mark, and squeezed it in hers.

"No, Aman. You're not in their power anymore. You don't have to be. You can still let emotion in. Aman . . ." Syah choked up. "I need you to *care*. Because I really, really want to be your friend." His eyes were focused on hers, but no emotion broke through.

Syah went on, feeling broken and exhausted. "I need you, Aman. I need someone who likes my art . . . someone who wants to create crazy worlds and stories with me. You're the only one I know who would do that."

Aman studied their joined hands. Then he said, "I didn't think I had any friends here. But you've been a better friend to me than even some of my old friends back home. I was scared people would laugh at me if they knew the real me. You didn't. You tried to help me, even though we just met. I think . . . maybe I can make other friends here too."

He looked up at Syah, and she saw her friend again. She smiled and squeezed his hand. When she let go, the mark of the Witchless was gone. Aman stared at his palm in amazement. Syah threw her arms around him in a giant hug, and her tears soaked into his coat. He hugged her back just as hard.

"I know it'll take a while to work through all of this, but I promise I'll help you on the way," Syah assured him. "Together we can figure out what will help you. With practice, you'll know what to do when you start to feel your anxiety taking over."

Aman hugged her tighter. "Thank you," he said into her hair. Syah felt so relieved to have him back.

Then she heard the magistrates and remembered they had been ready to *remove* her.

Syah let go and quickly faced the magistrates. They had stopped only a few feet away. They had reformed into their shimmering gray bodies. "We have decided," they said. "This new sentence is sufficient if the boy continues to carry it out."

Aman nodded instantly. "Yes. I will."

Syah reached out and took Aman's hand again. The pull of the Drift felt so strong she couldn't resist it. Syah thought of the emergency passphrase she had never spoken, satisfied to be ending the link naturally. *This is the true 'serenity,'* she thought as Aman's mindscape dissolved around them. Feeling relieved, she closed her eyes and rode the Drift back to reality.

CHAPTER 11

Aman — MindLink Lab, Emdaria North Middle School

Aman blinked in the bright white light of the MindLink lab. His body felt stiff and achy on the hard table. He sat up and was pulled back by something on his forehead.

"Oh! Hang on! Here," said the counselor as she hurried over to take the wires off Aman's temples.

To Syah, Aman heard her say, "Everything okay?" Syah nodded quickly, brushing her eyes with the back of her hand. "Good," the counselor said with a warning look. "That must have been quite the session. The MindLink machine readings were all over the place."

"Yeah," Syah admitted. "You could say that."

"Let me have some food brought in from the cafeteria while I get you both some passes. You missed lunch, and classes have already started again." The counselor hurried out of the lab to her office.

"I'm glad to see you're feeling better," the school nurse said to Aman. "If you need anything, please come and see me." Then she too left the room.

"Thanks," Syah called after her.

She looked at Aman sitting on the MindLink table across from her. He felt his face flush, and his breathing quickened. Everything suddenly felt strange. Would Syah abandon him now that she was free from his mind?

"Oh, no you don't!" Syah said, jumping off her table and hopping up to sit beside Aman. "Here, lie back. There's this ancient technique called *mindfulness* that I read about. It's like meditation. You focus only on the things that are happening right now, and nothing else."

Aman did as he was told.

Syah's voice was calm and soothing. "Here's one way it works. Close your eyes and pay attention to your breathing. How does it feel? What is the air like? Is it warm or cool? Feel your stomach move up and down as you breathe. Listen to your heart beating."

Aman tried to focus on what she said. Yet his thoughts kept swirling around. What would happen when he had to face people who had seen his panic attack in the middle of class? They'd think he was crazy.

Syah seemed to understand, because the next thing she said was spot on. "If your mind wanders, come back to the present. If you start thinking about your worries and fears or about what *might* happen, push those thoughts away. Just focus on *right now*. Think about what you can hear. What does it sound like? What can you feel? What are you touching? If your thoughts start to spin out of control, focus on your breathing. Keep it simple."

Aman did. *Breathe in—hold. Breathe out—hold. One. Breathe in—hold. Breathe out—hold. Two.* He kept his count and felt himself calm down. Then he followed Syah's suggestion and listened to the room. He heard the sound of air softly going in and out of his nose. He felt the leathery plastic table cushions beneath his fingers. He let go of the negative thoughts.

He didn't have to care what people thought. It might not be as easy, but he could be himself. He didn't have to fake being confident just so others wouldn't be uncomfortable around him.

He reached out, found Syah's hand, and squeezed it. She squeezed back. He opened his eyes and found that she was smiling. Aman smiled too. He could push past his dream monsters. He could take back control.

A bit timidly, he asked Syah, "So now you know what really goes on inside my head. Do you still want to illustrate my stories?"

"Ha!" Syah laughed. "Are you kidding? Now I know *exactly* what the crazy things in your stories might look like. I'm definitely up for that challenge! Didn't I say that you wouldn't get rid of me so easily?" She gave him a smirk. Aman closed his eyes and, for the first time, felt that he could be happy in Emdaria City.

ABOUT THE AUTHOR

Gina Kammer grew up in Narnia and Middle-earth, often writing and illustrating her own stories. Gina studied English at Bethany Lutheran College and took writing and theater courses in London. After earning her M.A. in Literature at the University of South Dakota, she edited a small-town newspaper. Now she edits children's books and occasionally teaches writing and journalism courses. When not writing, Gina loves reading science fiction, fantasy, and medieval literature. She also enjoys traveling, oil painting, archery, and snuggling her grumpy bunny. She lives in southern Minnesota with her husband and menagerie of critters. You can visit Gina online at ginakammer.com.

ABOUT THE ILLUSTRATORS

David Demaret is a freelance illustrator and concept artist living in Paris, France. He specializes in science fiction and heroic fantasy art. He comes from the video game industry with over twenty years of experience. As a senior graphic artist and art director, he worked on several well-known video games including: DUKE NUKEM 3D, DRIVER, KING KONG, LORD OF THE RINGS, GHOST RECON, COUNTERSTRIKE, LEGACY OF KAIN, DARK MESSIAH and BROTHERS IN ARMS. Since 2009, he has been focusing on illustrations and concept art as a new venture.

Chris Chalik was born in 1973 on the Polish-German border into a family with German and Russian roots. Since 2003 he has been living and working in London. His work is characterized by a dark and mysterious quality. He is co-author of SHADOW HEALER, a graphic novel published in the U.S. In 2011 his short comic story about the economy won third prize in a competition in Poland, organized for a well-known non-profit organization. He has had three exhibitions of his artwork in Poland.

TALK IT OVER

1. When Aman has a serious panic attack during class, Syah thinks an emergency MindLink session is the best way to help him. Do you think she was right? Why or why not?

2. Think about the various situations and thoughts that cause Aman anxiety. Are there any patterns? What causes Aman to suffer from the most anxiety?

3. When Syah enters the MindLink session with Aman she's excited to use what she learned about anxiety at Dr. Gables' workshop. She wants to prove that she can be just as good as the peer counselors at the high school. How do you think her goals change throughout the story?

4. Compare the technology found in Emdaria City with the city from Aman's mindscape. Discuss what makes the two cities similar or different.

THINK AND WRITE

1. During the story Aman often hides his feelings from other students. Pick a scene in which Aman is putting on an act and rewrite it from Syah's perspective. Then rewrite it from Aman's point of view. Try to show what he is really feeling as he puts on a brave face for others.

2. Pretend you are Aman. You've just come out of the MindLink session with Syah, but you still have to work hard at handling your anxiety. Write out a plan for the counselor of the things you'll work on and practice.

3. Aman's mom really hopes he'll become a scientist like her. She wants him to join science-related activities at his new school. Pretend you are Aman and write a letter to your mom. Tell her how you feel about science and how you'd like to do different activities instead.

4. Syah uses real methods that psychologists use to help people who struggle with anxiety. Write down three real-world ways you think might be useful for calming down, stopping a panic attack, or dealing with anxiety.

GLOSSARY

botany (BOT-uh-nee)—the scientific study of plants

coven (KUHV-uhn)—a group of witches, normally including thirteen individuals

hyperventilate (hahy-per-VEN-tih-layt)—to breathe uncontrollably fast and deep, often causing dizzyness

initiation (i-nish-ee-AY-shuhn)—a ceremony to bring someone into a club or group

magistrate (MAJ-uh-strayt)—an official who makes and enforces laws

paranoia (pair-uh-NOY-uh)—a mental disorder in which one has unreasonable thoughts or feelings that others mean to cause you harm

psychology (sye-KOH-luh-jee)—the study of the mind, emotions, and human behavior

simulation (sim-yuh-LAY-shuhn)—a recreation of something in real life, often done with a computer

subconscious (suhb-KON-shuhs)—the part of a person's mind in which mental processes occur without being aware of them

talisman (TAL-is-muhn)—an object believed to contain magical properties, often worn as an amulet or charm